CAN THIS MARRIAGE BE SAVED?

CAN THIS MARRIAGE BE SAVED?

A Memoir by

NANCY McCABE

UNIVERSITY OF MISSOURI PRESS

Columbia

Copyright © 2020 by
The Curators of the University of Missouri
University of Missouri Press, Columbia, Missouri 65211
Printed and bound in the United States of America
All rights reserved. First printing, 2020.

Library of Congress Cataloging-in-Publication Data

Names: McCabe, Nancy, 1962- author.
Title: Can this marriage be saved? : a memoir / by Nancy McCabe.
Description: Columbia, Missouri : University of Missouri Press, [2020]
Identifiers: LCCN 2020010709 (print) | LCCN 2020010710 (ebook) | ISBN
    9780826222121 (hardcover) | ISBN 9780826274472 (ebook)
Subjects: LCSH: McCabe, Nancy, 1962---Marriage. | McCabe, Nancy,
    1962---Childhood. | Women--United States--Biography. | Marriage--
    United States.
Classification: LCC CT275.M295 A3 2020 (print) | LCC CT275.M295
    (ebook) | DDC 977.8/043092 [B]--dc23
LC record available at https://lccn.loc.gov/2020010709
LC ebook record available at https://lccn.loc.gov/2020010710

♾™ This paper meets the requirements of the
American National Standard for Permanence of Paper
for Printed Library Materials, Z39.48, 1984.

Typefaces: Delicato Pro and Titular

CONTENTS

Contents

CAN THIS MARRIAGE BE SAVED?

Can This Marriage Be Saved? A Quiz

1. Which best describes your reasons for marrying him?

a. You have no idea. You were only twenty, too young to know what you were doing.

b. You have no idea. You were twenty, old enough to know better.

c. This is what you're trying to figure out. You weren't in love with him. You weren't even attracted to him, even though he was a perfectly nice person, clean and wiry, his prematurely receding hairline and thick brows and goofy humor reminding you of a Muppet, sweet and cartoonish. You felt toward him a fraternal affection.

d. You were trying to somehow fill the emptiness that came over you at dusk the months after your first love disappeared.

e. Marriage seemed like a healthier refuge than drugs or drinking. You imagined escaping into it, like going to sleep and waking up a new person.

f. Your husband-to-be cried the day he confessed to sleeping with an old girlfriend. You were in bed with the flu, and you thought, Oh, good. He'd brought you milkshakes and roses; he'd played endless rounds of gin rummy. But now he was saying, "I'm so sorry." You tried to shrug off the blankets, turn the pillow for a cool spot, but the bedclothes were weighed down by something: his head, burrowing into tousled sheets. That's when you realized he was crying, pinning covers against your feverish skin. "It's okay," you said, patting his head.

g. You were saddened by his anguish, seeing in it your own anguish over your first love, seeing in it all the world's unfulfilled longings.

h. He begged you to marry him, and you knew you would never get what you wanted, so why compound the grief by denying him what he wanted too?

i. One evening you fell asleep while he was fondling your breasts, and you woke to find him wearing your bra tied to his head like a bonnet. And you thought, I could do worse than wake up every morning to someone who makes me laugh.

j. You came from a chaotic home with junk mail piled all over the kitchen counter, tilted lampshades and crooked pictures, dead bugs speckling light covers, a necklace of Christmas bulbs along the roofline year-round. His parents' home was always cool, with deep, soft chairs, fans of *Architectural Digests* and *Home and Gardens* on the coffee table, thick carpets, polished floors, gin and tonics in small heavy glasses. You thought, I could do worse than be part of a family so much more refined than mine.

k. You were always reading the women's magazines your mother subscribed to, *McCall's, Good Housekeeping, Ladies' Home Journal,* which gave a nod to the idea that women now had careers and lives of their own, but still assumed that all women aspired to marriage and motherhood, valuing domestic life above all. That a home should be a safe haven, a tranquil respite from an impersonal world. You yearned for that. He might not be quite what you had envisioned as a life partner, but if you could have that refuge and peace, did it matter?

l. You thought, Won't I regret it if my heartlessness drives him away and there's never anyone else?

m. You knew that some part of you would always be out of his reach, a part that could never be touched or hurt, a part you could preserve just for yourself, and that seemed like a good thing after the devastating loss of your first love.

n. Your first love failed to reappear and execute a dramatic rescue at the altar, the kind in books and movies where right when you draw back a breath to say, "I do," he comes running up the aisle, or leaping from the balcony, or shouting at the window, and you pinch up the sides of your wedding gown and run to meet him.

o. You told yourself that after the wedding, by force of will, you would be attracted to your husband-to-be, that his touch would melt you and give you shivers at the same time, the way your first love's did.

p. All of the above.

q. None of the above.

r. You're too confused by the tangled mess you got yourself into. You have no idea.

THE GARDEN OF EARTHLY DELIGHTS

THE FIRST TIME I saw a slide of Hieronymus Bosch's *Garden of Earthly Delights* projected onto the screen in art history class, Marc and I had been married for nine months and I felt like I was viewing a metaphor for my own life. That painting somehow encapsulated the creepy, trapped feeling I'd had at my first college party, the first time I'd kissed Marc. The painting seemed to capture my unease about the direction my life had taken. I'd known it was a mistake to marry him, but for some reason I'd walked right into it.

The painting's central panel, with its pale, frail, writhing limbs and haunting juxtapositions of eggs and fruit, suggested a moral abandon that transformed, in the right panel, to the torments of hell. There, a man had been crucified in a harp, another shut up in a drum, slashed and confined as if in the grip of the same crushingly loud music I remembered from the party. Hell was an indecipherable world of shapes that might simultaneously be outer-space vegetables or disembodied ears, nebulous images that made no distinction between human and animal. I stared at the broken egg in the middle—or was it a dressed chicken, or a stomach ripped from a body's cavity?

I was mesmerized by what seemed to me a rendering of that Halloween party's similar confusion of inanimate, beast, and human, civilization as I thought I knew it giving way to the savagery of multicolored wigs and gauzy dresses, tails and masks and pointy ears. Why had I, given the desperation I'd felt at that party, married him anyway?

I'd been eighteen the night I found myself in the front seat of a car, wearing cardboard horns and a red jumpsuit, making out with a bearded man dressed like a nun. I found Marc's costume a little offensive, and I didn't like the way his hands groped my small breasts. His kisses were wet and sloppy and it grossed me out the way he kept sticking his tongue in my ear. I froze and pulled away, but he just followed, hiking up the tongue action.

How had I, a girl with a strict religious upbringing who'd recently been in love with a boy who wanted to be a priest, come to this? My mother, who'd grown up a Nazarene, forbidden to dance or go to movies because even ballroom dance could be too sensual and tickets to G-rated films supported pornography, had hoped I would attend a church college. "Maybe someday you'll go to college here," she'd said to me when we visited a cousin's dorm at Mid-America Nazarene College, a school where girls were only allowed to wear pants on the most bitterly cold days. She said the same thing when, on a family vacation, we ascended the prayer tower at Oral Roberts University in Oklahoma. I couldn't imagine applying to either of these colleges. I was by then growing more and more uncomfortable with their doctrine, but more importantly, I couldn't picture going to those places because they were hours from home and I was too afraid of the outside world, of being on my own.

And so, because I couldn't fathom leaving my home with its bug-speckled light covers and the iron fish symbol nailed to the front door that meant *Christians live here*, I was now a student at the local state university. That's where I'd met Marc, my boss at the student newspaper. He thought it was funny when, at work one day, I told him about the copy of *Cheaper by the Dozen* on our family room bookshelf; all of the *damns* had been blotted out by my mom back in the fifties when she'd read the book to her fifth graders. His family was much more lighthearted, fond of practical jokes, like the time his mom had spent months dropping clues suggesting that she was pregnant, then, when April rolled around, sent telegrams to everyone that said, "April fool!"

Marc didn't know quite what to make of me, but we were even, since I didn't know what to make of him either. I knew that the outside world was full of frightening, sordid people, drug addicts and hippies in short shorts and halter tops like those long-haired young people we saw at the Bluegrass Festival in Winfield, Kansas, or the pictures of teenagers in my Living Bible. "Hippie" was our all-purpose word for those types. My parents didn't officially disdain dancing, but in the presence of music, they tended to mimic the onset of rigor mortis. Among my aunts, a little toe-tapping to music was okay, but they all frowned at the shoulder-shimmying, hip-rotating abandon of hippie girls.

My whole childhood, I'd gone to church every Sunday and been a steady if somewhat lazy student and Campfire Girl who never bothered to do anything challenging to earn my beads. I didn't research African legends, make a marimba and play it in a rhythm orchestra, or construct a chemical hygrometer. Instead, I'd lit a candle, put it out by lowering a cup over it, and earned a bead for showing that fire couldn't burn without oxygen. The next month I'd obtained another bead by demonstrating a relaxation exercise, pretending to be a rag doll for three minutes.

I'd eventually quit Campfire Girls to join a Nazarene kids' club called Caravan, where I diligently memorized the Twenty-third Psalm from the King James Bible, with all of its *thous* and *preparests* and *anointests* and *runneths*. I didn't last long, never being promoted from Pathfinder to Cabin Helper, Camp Keeper, or the ultimate, Homemaker, but only because I had a falling-out with the friend who'd first invited me.

I was not the sort of girl who was raised to let guys grab at me in the front seats of their cars. But here I was without knowing quite why, except that I kept catching glimpses of my bangs and forehead in the rearview mirror, my transparent self in the windows, and I'd think, with wonder, That girl looks like a normal person, making out in a car. Not like an awkward girl dumped nine months ago by the love of her life. And so I stayed and didn't tell Marc to stop, because I thought that if I could pretend to be a normal person, eventually I would be one.

"You're so sexy in that costume." Marc pitched his veil and my horns into the back seat.

I looked at him skeptically. I was wearing a hideous double-knit red polyester jumpsuit that had been a last-minute purchase from the Goodwill store. I shrank into my bucket seat covered in fake fur, out of reach of Marc's hands and tongue.

Out the window, couples in garish makeup and rubber masks came and went from a disintegrating Victorian house with loose porch railings and cracked siding. Inside, it reeked of pot and cigarette smoke. Inside, Jimi Hendrix and Janis Joplin trembled the walls and people yelled over the music until they were hoarse. I wondered if anyone from the party had seen Marc feeling me up out here, and I shrank away from him even further, pressing myself against the window.

"What's wrong? I said you looked good," Marc protested.

"Don't make fun of me." I peeled hair, stiff with dried sweat, off my forehead. It ripped away like the sticky edges of a Band-Aid.

When we'd arrived an hour before, smoke already hung foglike over rooms with crumbling yellow carpet pads, big empty rooms with only a rickety kitchen chair here, a dingy mattress there. It was warm for late October and the windows were all shut tight, turning the air to a cloudy fishbowl. Music drummed from wall to wall. When people shouted, their mouths moved as soundlessly as goldfish trolling a bowl for flakes of food.

I tried to smile as a guy in a Groucho Marx nose sized me up, his gaze traveling from my knees up to my breasts and then flicking away, seeking out more impressive cleavage.

The music died down.

"Hot," said Luke Skywalker, voice loaded with irony as his eyes raked me.

Marc beamed proudly. "Bless you, my child," he told Luke Skywalker in falsetto. "Hail Mary full of grace."

I stabbed him with my pitchfork. I meant to be playful. My attempt felt strained.

A woman in a Playboy bunny outfit and fishnet stockings twitched her little round tail as she pranced by, casting me a scornful look.

The music blasted again. When had Halloween stopped being about pretend? I wondered as I threaded my way past a cat, a streetwalker, and Audrey Hepburn. When had it become an excuse for girls to wear clingy black things?

I'd never been in the presence of an illegal drug. When someone passed Marc a joint, he pinched it between two fingers and sucked at it, then tried to relay it to me. I shook my head.

Marc looked a little abashed at my discomfort. On the second round, he passed. And then whispered, "Let's get out of here."

That's when we'd escaped into the crisp fall air, where an enormous wave of grief for my high school boyfriend swept over me. Being in love with him felt like I'd lost my senses, literally, like I barely noticed anything but him, the expressions on his face, the sound of his voice. When I'd been in love, I'd never gulped in fresh air as thankfully as I did now, or noticed the way falling leaves surfed the breeze and rustled against each other as they landed, a constant shivering bustle that made it sound like it was always raining. I could still hear the murmur of leaves, sitting there in the car, away from the music that had pulsed through me like a headache.

Partying, it seemed to me, was designed to block the senses, to make everyone high and deaf and blind in the smoky air, and for no good reason. At least love had been a good reason to shut out the rest of the world. I couldn't imagine feeling the way I'd felt about my first love ever again. But the last few weeks, when I'd caught Marc's intense dark eyes watching me across the college paper newsroom, I'd thought he was a sincere person, above false compliments and calculating lines. I'd liked him, but I hadn't wanted to go out with him.

Now, remembering, I felt guilty about this. I smiled a guilty tentative smile. That's all the encouragement Marc needed to descend on me once again, tugging at the zipper down my front.

"Don't," I said. Maybe, when we'd first left the party, I'd felt a brief hope that I could enjoy making out with someone who wasn't my high school boyfriend, but now I knew that I couldn't.

"Don't you like me?" Marc asked.

"Yes." I held his hands so he couldn't unzip me. He looked cheerful, as if he were interpreting this restraining gesture as a sign of affection.

"Don't you trust me?" he asked.

I wasn't sure, only that I'd been flattered by his attention, which made me feel guilty, which drove my niceness up a few notches. I couldn't tell him I wasn't really attracted to him. I really wanted to be attracted to him. If I tried hard enough, I thought I could force myself to be.

"Just relax," Marc whispered.

"We hardly know each other," I said. "Let's just talk."

His habit tangled as he fell with exasperated exaggeration against the back of his seat. "Okay," he said. "Talk."

"No, you."

"Talk about what?" He stared at my breasts.

I turned slightly to obstruct his view. "Why do you hold your back like that?" I asked. I had been wondering a long time why he carried himself so straight, moving carefully, a little stiff.

He gave me a funny look. "I have a disease called ankylosing spondylitis. It's kind of like arthritis in my spine."

"Really?" Suddenly I felt tender toward him. Suddenly, I saw him differently, as someone with depth and courage and experience and wisdom. With my fingertips, I lightly stroked the thick hair on his arm, wondering it if could

13

change directions like a cat's fur, revealing a glistening underside.

"It was awful when it started," he said. "I was sixteen. I'd get out of bed in the morning and my legs would collapse under me. I spent two years on pain pills before a doctor diagnosed it. It was the reason I kept dropping out of school. I worked as a carpenter for a long time, but I can't really do that long-term, even though the last few years have been okay physically."

I squeezed his hand.

"One of my uncles has it. His spine froze and he ended up in a wheelchair," Marc said. "That could happen to me too."

He watched me anxiously as if he expected me to be repelled by this revelation, but instead I found myself warming toward him. Maybe he seemed different from the other guys I knew not just because at twenty-six, he was eight years older than me, but because suffering had deepened and matured him.

"I think I love you," he said suddenly, hopefully, and I knew exactly where he was going with that.

"I'm not having sex till I'm married," I replied.

My words had the desired effect. His hand, inching toward my zipper, stilled in midair, then dropped.

"You're such a strange person," he said.

For the first time ever, I felt completely comfortable with him. "I know," I said. "That's why you like me."

"I think I want to marry you," he joked, still looking hopeful.

I laughed uneasily and slipped back in my seat, putting distance between us again. Out the window, leaves tap-danced, shuffling on the asphalt, then hop-stepping and kicking up in the wind. This street, where just a few hours ago children had trick-or-treated, now was desolate. For a second, marriage seemed weirdly appealing—not marriage to Marc, just marriage in the abstract, as if it could be a refuge from the scary and unpredictable and unfathomable world. I imagined, fleetingly, a life where I'd be insulated from smoky rooms and throbbing music and people in masks whose identities I couldn't determine, whose expressions I couldn't read, from drugs and violence and terrifying realities. But I quickly regained my senses, at least temporarily.

"I'm never getting married," I said, and at the time, I thought I meant it.

Can This Marriage Be Saved? A Quiz

2. True or False: You sometimes feel like you don't really exist.

a. Wait a minute—isn't this a question from the Minnesota Multiphasic Personality Inventory? What does it have to do with your marriage?

b. False. As a child, on a swing, the wind rushing by, your stomach lifting and dropping, you used to think, with a little thrill, I'm alive. I exist. I exist, you used to think, and the thought caused you to exist in that moment the way the world magically existed when God said, "Let there be light" and there was light.

c. True. Sometimes you suspected that the world was a cosmic joke everyone else was in on but you. What if nobody else really existed and you didn't either and any day they'd all tell you the truth? "Surprise!" they'd exclaim, springing out from behind trees and bushes. Your existence, it would turn out, was an elaborate experiment, an illusion, a source of someone else's entertainment.

d. False. You always had a strong sense of self. Your parents like to tell a story about how when you were three, on vacation in Galveston, you begged to participate in a program at your hotel called Operation Kidnap. Your parents had initially pitched it to your four-year-old brother: "Wouldn't that be fun?" they asked him. He would swim in the hotel pool with other kids and do crafts and go to the beach for a sandcastle-building contest. He adamantly refused, but you piped up, "I want to go." They reluctantly agreed. You gave them permission to check up on you during the day, then added, "But you have to pretend you don't know me." This would become ingrained in family lore, evidence of how independent you have always been, evidence of how little you needed them, even at three.

e. True. You begged your parents to enroll you in preschool because you were jealous of your brother who started kindergarten at four, another sign of your bravery, your independence. But one day you overheard a teacher say, "Nancy is a very timid child." You won't remember the context of this, only that you didn't know what the word *timid* meant and so you held onto this overheard comment for the years it took to find out. And wondered which you were. Brave and independent, or shy and timid? Did the inconsistency somehow cancel you out, make you nebulous, impossible to define?

f. False. You grew up in a neighborhood where a serial killer was on the loose, and you were terrified that something terrible would happen to you, terrified at the way murder took away people altogether. You were terrified at the idea of not existing anymore.

g. True. You felt like an object as hollow and disposable as a plastic bottle or a Styrofoam cup the day eight boys cornered you in a lab classroom. The details blurred: a snapped bra, groping hands, a fly unzipping, moaning, howling, vacant eyes, snarled teeth. You were caged but they were the animals. When a teacher's footsteps approached, there was a hum of zippers, like a high-pitched invasion of bees, as the boys shoved you aside and fled. You remained, shaking and askew, at a black-topped table meant for dissecting the delicate tissues and organs of something that was once alive.

h. False. When your first love looked at you, you were no longer a ghost. It didn't make sense to you: he was an unlikely hero, scrawny, with plumped-up lips it took him a few years to grow into, a skinny, quiet boy with silky dark hair and long fingers. He wanted to be a priest or a monk, but he changed his career goals and gave you his father's class ring, so big you had to tape around it twenty times to make it fit your finger. He scribbled in the margin of your class notes, "Hello my honey, hello my baby, hello my sweetie pie. What am I going to do? I'm in love with you." You came across his scrawl while studying, and you existed.

i. True. You took refuge in marriage and then felt as if you'd erased yourself from the earth.

j. All of the above.

WAYS TO TELL A STORY

EVERY MORNING WHEN I'm small, I wait for God to wake up. I can hear Him, as the dawn diffuses darkness and the upper edge of the sun breaks through the horizon. I picture it like a kind of reversal of gravity, an egg yolk bursting upward through its shell. A distant groan, small and whiny as a pesky fly, builds gradually into a majestic crashing roar. The sound explodes, rattling the windows and the dishes in the cupboards. It's a strange harmony, the overpowering thundering almost drowning the eerie jangle of glass. The house's foundation quivers and I put my hands over my ears to shut out the booming, half-fearing that the house will topple and shatter into a million splinters. And then, always, the relief of the sound retreating into the distance, dying away, leaving my world intact.

I think of this as the sound of morning. I imagine God in His heavens, yawning and stretching the earth into place, expanding it from a tiny dark ball to the light daytime world, blaring out reminders of his eternal presence and his almighty benevolence. I retain this image of a thunderous morning God until I am at least nine or ten or eleven years old.

I live in a neighborhood bordered on two sides by major highways, cut off at one end by the Kansas turnpike, and poised directly under the flight pattern of McConnell Air Force Base. This land once belonged to a farm. Remnants include rickety wooden footholds up the side of a tree along the deepest part of the creek, where dirt clots the hairy roots that hang above eroded banks. I often play in an old dump at the back of a field among the rubble of an overturned rusty car, a discarded toilet, and sandpaper-rough squares of old shingles. Our street's newer houses, ranches and split levels, sit back from the road, with long gravel driveways and no sidewalks. It is not a neighborhood designed for evening strolls, dog walking, or gossiping with neighbors.

Our house is like a checkerboard, two sides pale pink, two sides baby blue, because my dad once started to paint it but never finished. Old cars rust in our yard, infested by mice, fringes of weeds poking up into the grills. Christmas bulbs remain strung along the roofline because my dad never gets around to taking them down. I don't think of this as a sign of neglect so much as a demonstration of my parents' virtue, their lack of interest in material things;

after all, we are an upright family, pillars of our church community. On Sundays when we thread through the foyer, others fall silent and nod respectfully as we make our way to the back pew, where we stand stiffly through the service, never singing the hymns.

My dad works for Boeing Military Aircraft, but when I ask him what he does, he says only, "It's top secret." It is so top secret, officials from the Department of Defense must be stationed in the room if he has surgery. It is so top secret, he is prohibited from traveling to Communist countries. It is so top secret, he won't even tell me the name of his job, though many years later I will conclude, "So you're an electrical engineer?"

"Well, no, my degree is in math and physics," he'll respond, ever elusive.

On Saturdays, God roars, our house stirs, and screen doors creak on hinges, then bang shut. My dad and younger brother shovel flower beds, dirt like fresh growths of werewolf stubble on their hands and faces. My older brother fortresses himself in front of cartoons with comic books and cereal. His eyes ice over like frozen ponds and his jaw slackens. I hate the sound of the TV, the idea that somewhere else, not here, lives are being lived. I hate TV so much that I refuse to watch it, except for occasional afternoon sitcom reruns and *The Brady Bunch* on Friday night. My aversion to TV means that I have pretty much missed the entire Vietnam War; I wouldn't even know it existed if it weren't for the POW bracelets some of my classmates wear. I'm busy reading, mostly books about girls, like *Anne of Green Gables* and the Little House books and the Betsy-Tacy series. In many girls' books, the heroines have expressive faces and wild imaginations. They always meet the true loves of their lives by the time they're sixteen, even if they don't know it yet. I file all of this away. I like that Betsy and Anne want to be writers. I want to be a writer too.

In the basement, immune to craggy walls and cement floors, sewing machine whirring, my mother affixes piping to a new pantsuit. She makes all of our clothes, absorbed in her own world of leisure suits and turtleneck T-shirts, smocked blouses and bell-bottom pants, clothes I don't think much about until I emerge into the outside world and realize that I look a little bit different, a little bit odd in my homemade clothes compared to everyone else in their store-bought shirts and jeans and dresses. Once, finding cloth covered with big yellow smiley faces, she made matching overalls for my little brother and me. She deemed my big brother too old and dignified for overalls, so she made him bell-bottomed smiley face pants. Somehow, all of those sunny yellow smiley faces made me even crankier than usual.

My dad and little brother come in and cartoons give way to football. The hushed tension of the announcer and the windlike rise and fall of cheering crowds makes me feel, again, left out of someone else's fun. I hide out in my room. I love my room. I can read and dream there for hours, watching sunlight traverse the walls. Come night I will turn off the light and then take a running leap into my bed so the monster underneath it won't be able to reach out and grab my foot, but during long Saturdays as the light outside brightens then mellows, I feel safe and self-contained. I have moments of deep peace in solitude.

But my little brother beats on my door. He wants to show me a picture he's painted. It looks ruined to me because of the red watercolor he accidentally splattered across the strips of blue sky and green grass and the wide-armed leafy trees. I try to sympathize but then I see he's proud of his creation. "This is the way things look right after you look at the sun," he explains. "You know, with all of those dots in front of your eyes."

I'm impressed at how easily he believes that he can say a thing and make it so. I'm impressed at the idea that there's more than one way to interpret a mistake or tell a story.

He won't go away and let me read my book. He's pretending to be a cat and wants me to pet him. He annoys me like crazy yet still I love him with the kind of fierce, overwhelming love that makes me afraid I will squish newborn kittens. I fend off that terrifying intensity. "Go away," I tell him, and when he doesn't, I accuse him of being a baby and a brat.

Now his feelings are hurt. Guilty, anxious to protect him from myself, I say in a shocked, sweet, Nice-Nancy tone, "Was that Mean Nancy here?" I ply him with kisses. He goes away, bewildered by my inconsistency.

I emerge from my room only to make a sandwich for lunch. My older brother and I get into some dumb argument and then he starts trying to trip me up in my own sentences.

"Yes means no and no means yes," he says, as if he and he alone has the power to shift the whole English language. "Are you stupid?"

I refuse to answer. If I say no, it's supposed to mean yes, but if I say yes, he'll crow, "You are!"

I retreat outside, to the swing. I forget that I have rejected my little brother's efforts to connect with me and instead am grumpy about being the odd one out in my family, with two parents and two brothers and no sisters. My mom and dad always take each other's side, my older brother is my mom's favorite and my younger brother is her baby, and my dad finds me spacey while my brothers are always asking the kinds of questions that he approves of: Why the sky is blue, why the grass is green. How a radio works and why a fly in a moving car doesn't get smashed against the back window. On Family Day at Boeing, we tour airplanes and my brothers ask questions about electronics and aerodynamics.

I lapse into daydreams on the swing. Sometimes I hum songs under my breath, songs we sing on the school bus and songs I have learned from my cousins: morbid and disgusting ones about gopher guts, about worms that play pinochle on the toes of corpses, about "my dead dog Rover that I overran with the mower." The school bus driver won't let us sing "100 Bottles of Beer on the Wall." Instead, we sing "100 Bottles of Milk on the Wall." She doesn't object to "Heigh-ho, heigh-ho, it's off to school we go / with razor blades and hand grenades," or

Glory, glory hallelujah,
teacher hit me with a ruler.
Met her at the door with a loaded .44,
and she ain't my teacher no more.

I sing these songs and imagine living in an airplane, sleeping above the wing. The songs are fun and ridiculous because this kind of violence is so unimaginable. Sure, there is violence in the world, but it's far, far away, in countries whose names I don't know. I'm immune to all that while I imagine fixing grilled peanut butter sandwiches in the kitchenette of my airplane while I fly through the sky.

I swing, wishing I could fly away. I live on Greenwich Road in Wichita, words pronounced so that they are full of witches. I imagine that the street in front of our house is a witch's broomstick, the nearby turnpike hill is her humped back, and I am the product of some mysterious spell. I have learned in Sunday school that witches are bad, even the kind in *Bewitched*, so bad they won't inherit the kingdom of God.

I swing, pretending I am a witch soaring through the clouds.

In Wichita, the Air Capital of the World, because of level ground and scarce fog, half the world's airplanes are built. My childhood friends later will recall the endless noise of planes taking off from McConnell Air Force Base for Vietnam. The growl and hum and then the thunder of planes is the backdrop to my childhood. They pass low, scaring rabbits back into their burrows, urging flocks of restless birds into startled flight, momentarily halting lessons in classrooms, postponing intimate confessions, scrawling secret messages in contrails across the sky.

In the yard, I swing among trees barely taller than I am, their branches still twigs. The swing creates a breeze, a rush of wind, a lift and drop in my stomach as I glide into the cloudless sky and then am pulled back toward the earth. I plan my jump, at the apex of the swing's trajectory. I will let go of the chains, will propel myself through the air, will land on my feet. I imagine it, but am too luxuriously lazy to let go.

And then, so high that the chain jerks and the swing set jumps a little from the ground, yanked down abruptly and pumping my way up again, I think, suddenly, *I'm alive.*

A small shivery breeze ripples through me.

I exist, I think and the hairs stand up on my arm the way the wind stirs the grass.

The miracle of my existence fills me with happiness. The sun filters through clouds and warms my skin, the swing pushes me toward the sky.

I'm alive. I exist.

I know what it was like when God said, "Let there be light" and there was light. *I exist*, I think, and I exist.

Back in the house, I run into my older brother, retrieving chips from the kitchen.

"I means you and you means me," I say, triumphant. Two can play his game. "So earlier, you were saying you were stupid?"

"If I means you and you means me, you just said that you're the one who's stupid," my brother says.

"You just said you were," I answer.

"Stop calling yourself stupid," he says, and all tangled up in words and rage, I lash out. "I hate you," I say.

My mother appears from the hall, snapping out of her habitual distraction. "Don't ever say that," she rebukes me. "The Bible says that anyone who hates his brother is a murderer."

My big brother smiles smugly.

Leafing through the Bible, I'm increasingly indignant. I can find no verses protecting sisters.

And worse, God always seems to play favorites with siblings, pitting them against each other. What's the deal with God rejecting Cain's offering of fruit while preferring Abel's portions of firstborn lambs? How come Jacob gets away with making off with Esau's birthright and their father's blessing? God even seems to offer tacit approval, saying, "Yet I loved Jacob, and I hated Esau, and laid his mountains and his heritage waste for the dragons of the wilderness." Disappointingly, my Sunday school teacher explained that there were no actual dragons at the time, and that newer translations say *jackals*, not *dragons*.

I get why after murdering his brother, Cain is doomed to be a restless wanderer on the earth, but leaving Esau's inheritance to the desert jackals? Is that really fair?

The story of Mary and Martha really makes me tense. Martha does all the cooking and cleaning to make Jesus comfortable while Mary just hangs out with him pouring perfume on his feet and wiping them with her hair, which sounds pretty gross, and then Jesus says completely unnecessarily that he likes Mary better.

I'm afraid that I'll always be the one who doesn't fare well, the one given to murderous rages, the one whose mountains are wastelands, the workhorse with a sense of dignity too pervasive to smear perfume all over any Messiah's stinky feet.

Not to mention that I am allergic to perfume.

Should I be comforted because Rachel, the beautiful wife of Jacob, ends up unable to have babies, while her weak-eyed underdog of a sister is given all the children? So that's her reward—wearing glasses and having a whole bunch of babies? Babies are cute, but my little brother is exhausting enough to take care of, and giving birth sounds painful.

I go outside and walk, walk off my anger and turmoil, wading through the tall grass of the empty field across the street to the old farm dump. Recently, a classmate told me that a lion had escaped from the Sedgwick County Zoo. Or maybe it's a circus the lion escaped from, or a zoo somewhere else. Or maybe it's just something I made up.

I become so lost in pondering what's real and what's my imagination that I forget to be mad.

I pretend that the upside-down, rusted-out car with empty wheel wells is a house. The car's underside is the upstairs, with bumps and ridges for couches and chairs. Old shingles resemble bread charred in a broiler. I pretend it's toast. I shade my eyes, gazing out beyond the car's dented bumper, scanning the horizon for wild rampaging lions.

Maybe I'm in danger. Maybe an escaped lion will leap right up on top of that upside-down car and attack me. The high grass of the field ripples like a powerful mane. Maybe I'm afraid, or maybe I'm not, instead imagining myself as a member of the Swiss Family Robinson, washed up on an unfamiliar shore. Except, instead of a treehouse, I have an upside-down car, and instead of wild berries, I have burnt toast, and instead of jungle animals, I have a lion that might have escaped from the zoo.

Home again, I don't want to go in, so I swing again. I think the words again, *I'm alive, I exist*. A jagged thrill zippers through me. But then I brush my feet in the dirt, slowing down, wondering. What if the world is actually a big joke everyone is in on but me? What if it's just some kind of illusion created to see how gullible I am? What if no one really exists and I don't either and one day they'll all tell me the truth? But then, if existence is just a trick being played on me, that would make me the center of the universe, and I'm pretty sure I'm not.

So I pump myself back into the air, soaring so high that I imagine the swing set will topple over, or the chains will wrap themselves around the upper bar and I will rotate round and round it like a planet around the sun, becoming hopelessly entangled. But still I swing higher and higher, testing out those words again: *I'm alive. I exist.*

Years later, I will visit Cave Hill Cemetery in Louisville, Kentucky, and a monument to a three-year-old girl called "Jesus Is My Swing Set." Young Sami died when she rode her trike into the family swimming pool, and now a somewhat wizened-looking likeness of her sits atop a wooden plank suspended by ropes gripped by the legless torso of a delighted Jesus. Stones on either side feature, in addition to little brass birds congregating around a miniature birdbath, the lyrics to Sami's favorite song, "Jesus Loves Me," the "O" shaped into a heart.

In this haunting poignancy of excess, I will remember my own childhood self, swinging, despite my dawning irritation at the Bible, still in the grip of Jesus back before the inevitable toppling of my vague notions. Before my mom calls me in to dinner and the TV channel turns to Lawrence Welk. Before a neighbor boy makes a comment about our junky yard and suddenly as we wind through the church foyer I note downward-cast eyes that seem more pitying than intimidated at the sight of my silent family in homemade clothes and I think, *We're weird. Tacky.* I know the world is round, that you can't walk right off the edge of it into eternal free-fall, but it feels like it, standing on the edge of that revelation.

That afternoon when I swing into the sun, it is years before I will announce to my dad that I've decided I'm a pacifist. "You don't know what you're talking about," my dad, by then a deacon at church and a leader in a national Bible study organization, will reply in a strangled voice. In Sunday school I've always heard that we should turn the other cheek, but my dad will be offended by my insistence that Jesus was a pacifist. My dad will tell me that my interpretation is simplistic, that I don't have enough life experience to have an informed opinion. He'll talk in a slow, patient voice that seems to mask intense agitation. He'll talk about World War II and Korea and Vietnam and his own years in the Navy. I'll respond feebly. He'll follow up with a thorough, well-reasoned argument each time I speak until finally I give up, understanding that I'm completely, hopelessly wrong, but deep down, pretty sure I'm still a pacifist.

I'll vow that someday I will have the skills to win a fight with him. And then, still more years later, he'll retire and hang on the wall of his study government citations for his work with electronic warfare, and I will understand for the first time that he didn't spend his career wiring reading lamps and flight attendant call buttons.

Periodically, during my childhood, people write to the *Wichita Daily Eagle* to complain that the noise of planes overhead invades their privacy, waking them in the night or altering their dreams.

"Thank the Good Lord for these 'Sleep Disturbers,'" writes someone signed "Loyal American." "I am wondering how much sleep that woman would get if those planes that so rudely awakened her at 2:00 a.m. belonged to our enemies. When I hear those planes, I have a feeling of security and pride."

And so, while others thank the Good Lord for the planes, I maintain my amorphous idea that those early morning planes lighting out for Vietnam are the Good Lord. Until a visiting cousin puts her hands over her ears while the house and the earth and the sky around us vibrate violently, and says, "What is that?" and pulls back the curtain, then loses interest. "Oh," she says. "It's just a plane."

Before any of that, though, I swing, briefly suspended there in childhood. I fly toward light, rising toward my real life, the one I will someday live elsewhere, a life that is only a faint vision still insulated from knowledge of war or destruction or death. I swing and feel renewed. I am Eve in Eden, suddenly alive, fully formed, awed by the fact of her existence. In the center of the garden she must have believed that all her sorrows would be healed, her eyes opened, in those moments before she became aware of how her ribs formed a cage.

FACTS ABOUT THE MOON

MY SEVENTH-GRADE SCIENCE textbook diagrams the two sides of the moon. There's the side that can be seen, mapped in detail by astronomers, and there's the moon's hidden side, photographed by a Russian satellite. Illustrations depict waterless seas, oceans, lakes, craters, and mountains. There's the Sea of Serenity and the Sea of Tranquility. There are also the Ocean of Storms and the Sea of Crises, and, always full of turmoil, I'm afraid that's where I'd live if I lived on the moon.

But I live far from any sea, in a small city on Earth, and sometimes I feel like the weirdest kid here. I've just started junior high after attending an elementary school in the country, and my clothes are all wrong, cheap—pale, easily wrinkled jeans and homemade shirts with yokes or embroidered flowers. My hair is long and always messy, waving in all the wrong directions. The girls I go to school with have Dorothy Hamill wedges or Farrah Fawcett shags and floral sundresses over scoop-necked T-shirts. They wrinkle their noses at me as if I am, by comparison, coarse and unwashed.

I don't know what things mean, words like *virgin* and *gay*. Because I rarely watch TV, I am somewhat oblivious to current events. Until a few years ago, I was unaware of things like the Vietnam War, popular music, or the existence of curse words. Entering junior high has been like hatching into a world that others have inhabited forever, and I walk around, bewildered, through the school's three connected circular buildings. From a distance, these buildings perch on the prairie like flying saucers that have just landed. Inside them, I walk in circles feeling like an alien in my increasingly unfamiliar body.

A couple of years ago, four members of the Otero family were murdered in their home in east Wichita. There were no signs of forced entry or struggle, though the whole family had been trained in judo. The phone lines had been cut. One of the victims was a girl just a year younger than I was.

I turned quickly past diagrams on the front page of the newspaper showing where each family member had been discovered, to the comics, but not before I saw that the girl was found hanging from a pipe in the basement.

Someone in the Otero family must have really pissed someone off, my classmates said. It made everyone feel safer to believe the family was somehow at fault. If that were true, we ourselves would be exempt from such senseless violence. But later that spring, nearby, an assailant strangled a young woman named Kathryn Bright and shot her brother, who survived. Did they piss someone off too?

I try to avoid the news, the details of these murders. I try to keep them at the periphery of my knowledge. But I still bolt up perspiring from nightmares, listening hard to every sigh and creak of the sleeping house.

In health class we study the reproductive system but don't talk about sex. My mother, though, decides when I am trapped in the car with her that it is time to fill me in. She worries constantly, usually aloud, that I'll be raped, hit by a car, coerced by a cult, converted by an atheist, or worst of all, impregnated. But today, she focuses on explaining the mechanics of sex and the importance of resisting lines like, "You would if you loved me." She tells me about the categories of girls: the ones guys marry and the ones guys make out with in the back seats of cars. She doesn't mention a third category, girls so freakish that they are completely ignored.

She warns me about diseases that promiscuous women can contract and about how teen pregnancy can blight a once-bright future. She tells me that many women wait to use tampons until after marriage so they don't lose their virginity. My curiosity has not surpassed my embarrassment, and I squirm uncomfortably, face ablaze, wishing desperately that she'd stop. Since I've never even kissed a boy, I'm sure that my mom is being sadistic, mocking me, giving me advice meant only to highlight my abnormality. I might as well live on the moon, hundreds of thousands of miles from ordinary life, so removed does all of this feel from my own experience.

I'm in eighth grade when the serial killer strikes again. He locks three children in a bathroom, and they thud against the door and scream as he strangles their mother, Shirley Vian. Wichitans install security systems, enroll in self-defense classes, buy guns, and keep bats and bricks by beds and doors. Every night my dad goes from door to door, checking all the locks, but my parents would, I think, roll their eyes if I revealed to them how afraid I am. I understand the treachery of thinking too much of myself, of believing that I matter enough to be endangered, assaulted, murdered, or singled out in any way that could make the news.

My eighth-grade bus route includes kids from the trailer court across Highway 54. They brag about causing bloodshed and broken bones, modify most nouns with the word *fucking*, and threaten to beat up anyone who offends them. In subzero temperatures, preferably during ice storms, they instigate games of Freeze Out. This consists of rolling down all the windows and stripping to their T-shirts to prove they aren't pussies. Being a pussy, I conclude, is akin to being a sissy. The word *sissy* seems to connect cowardice to being a girl, but it takes me a while to understand that the word *pussy* is also somehow related to girls, to the female anatomy.

I don't care whether I'm a sissy or a pussy or a coward. I just don't want to be cold. I zip my coat, tug down my stocking cap, and unfold my sweater's cowl to my chin. When a boy attempts to lower my window, I push his hands away.

"Are you a pussy?" asks the boy, whose face is purple with acne, his once-white undershirt gray.

"I'm just not stupid," I say, hearing an intake of breath around me.

The boy scoots sideways to look at me. I brace myself, waiting for him to curse me or punch me. Instead, after a long, tense moment, he says, "Want me to beat anyone up for you?"

In the science classroom, homemade mobiles of the solar system and models of planets hang from every light fixture, leftover projects from last year's classes. Gazing up at a Styrofoam and foil mobile demonstrating the moon's phases, I think maybe everyone is like the moon, with a side other people see and another, darker side full of secrets. My friends from elementary school are drifting away and I feel increasingly awkward and shy and unable to fit in anywhere, in my own hidden phase. As new and crescent and gibbous moons rustle gently against each other in air from the heating vent, I feel as if I too am becoming more crescent, obscured by shadows. All is silent on the moon, I remember reading. There is no air to carry sound waves.

Sometimes I eavesdrop on my mother and aunts talking. One of them tells a story about a friend of her daughter's who was sitting on the couch in a strange apartment, having just put the children she was babysitting to bed. Suddenly, the front door flew open and a naked man burst in. He looked lost and confused.

She screamed. He ran. My aunt says that when the police came, they asked, "Was he erect?"

"No," the girl answered. "He was just kind of leaning against the doorframe."

My mother and aunts laugh and laugh. I'm not sure what's so funny. Recently, my mom read "The Owl and the Pussycat" to her third-grade class. The kids kept giggling. My mom said to me, indignantly, "I don't get kids nowadays. To me a pussy will always be a cat and gay will always mean happy." I ponder all of this, starting to understand that words like *pussy* and *gay* and *erect* all have something to do with sex, although I'm not entirely clear what.

Diagrams on the walls of the science classroom plot the average distance of the planets from the sun, which represents home plate. Saturn is on second base, six other planets range around the infield, and Pluto skulks in the outfield. Another diagram shows relative sizes. If the sun is a beach ball, the smallest planets are the size of a pinhead, Uranus and Neptune are marbles, Saturn is a Ping Pong ball, and Jupiter is a golf ball.

The Styrofoam and foil planets that hang from the light fixtures are just the right size for a makeshift volleyball game during the midmorning half-hour activity period. My class is mostly boys, with only a couple of girls. One of the guys takes down Venus and we start batting it over the neon lights that hang from the ceiling. I'm good at light-fixture volleyball. "Good one," the boys yell when I slam Venus, clapping my back, and for the first time this year, I feel like I fit in.

This is the first year of co-ed gym. Co-ed gym is nothing like light-fixture volleyball. None of the elementary school activities I loved and was good at—three-legged races, scooter tag, square dancing, Ping Pong—are a part of co-ed gym. We play hard-core games, soccer and baseball and, worst of all, bombardment. Sometimes, during bombardment, it seems that the boys are out for blood. If I could, I'd be a gym conscientious objector.

The coach keeps yelling at me. "You're supposed to avoid the ball," he screams after I maneuver into the path of one so I can exit the game and daydream on the sidelines. I'm relieved to escape those balls heaved like weapons hard enough to leave bruises. A couple of weeks later, the coach hollers at me for ducking away from the ball in volleyball. I have it backward. I'm supposed to avoid the ball in bombardment and make contact with the ball in volleyball. Where is my fighting spirit? the coach asks me. How do I expect to survive life without a killer instinct?

In science, we study Latin terms and prepare to dissect frogs in the biology lab next to our classroom. "Plato thorax," the boys call me, which according to our vocabulary guide means "flat chest." You can't win: the girl who sits by me and has developed breasts gets called "Silicone Sister." The boys snap her bra when she's not looking.

The teacher is always stepping out of the classroom to run errands or take calls, leaving us to work independently. Once, deep in thought, I look up to find a boy standing in front of me with his pants unzipped, wiggling his privates. I look away, remembering the word *erect* from my aunt's story, how it seemed to imply some kind of danger. All of the boys cheer this boy on. They moan and hoot and shout profanities. "Gross," another girl says.

And then a new, unexpected thing starts happening in science class. I'm not sure what to call it. *Teasing* is too mild a word. The teacher leaves the room and the boys circle around me. They grab at me and yell obscenities. I'm so startled the first time it happens, I just stare at them, confused, trapped in the middle of a hooting mob.

"There are these boys that bother me," I tell my mother, and she smiles knowingly and says, "That means they like you." *Bother* is clearly not the right word either. But it's not rape or murder, and I don't know any words for anything in between. I don't yet know terms like *sexual harassment*, nor do I understand that as one of the few girls in the class and quite possibly the weirdest, I am intruding on a male space. For now, I worry that I have some terrible flaw that is attracting this attention.

"I'm glad I'm not you," one of the other girls says to me.

After one of these episodes, I stare up at the Styrofoam planets dangling from the ceiling. Limp string hangs down where Venus used to be; not long before, the foil peeled away from it and the Styrofoam crumbled in my hands during light-fixture volleyball. I focus on the remaining planets. I want to stretch up, touch Mars, as if touching it might transport me there.

One of my bus mates stabs his stepmother to death, and the other kids fill me in on unprinted details. He put his stepmother in the bathtub to drain her blood, then hid her under a bed and invited the neighbor kids in to have a look at his handiwork.

"Holy fucking shit," they said and notified the police.

The *Wichita Beacon* quotes the boy's teachers. "He seemed like a normal quiet guy," they say.

"He was planning it for fucking months," my bus mates say.

I'm no longer afraid of these people who are so upfront in their hostilities. Either they kill you outright, I think, or they leave you alone, unlike the boys in my science class. I have no idea what the label is for their treatment of me. They aren't beating me up, hurting me, attacking or assaulting me, are they? I think about the space rocks that pummeled the moon's surface billions of years ago, about how craters are really the scars that remain. Nothing all that bad is happening to me, so why do I feel so bad?

At lunch a guy passes by my table, cowboy hat tilted rakishly over one eye. He pauses to fondle himself and groan. Boys around the cafeteria hoot, whistle, and yelp. A teacher leans against the wall, arms folded, laughing. I know that if this gets any further out of hand, teachers are not the ones to go to for help.

"Mike says he raped you in biology class," says one of my elementary school friends, laughing. "He says you're going to go talk to your guidance counselor."

I have actually been thinking about talking to the counselor, but now that this possibility has been turned into a joke, I can't imagine being seen going into her office.

"Are those boys still bothering you?" my mom asks, looking amused. Sometimes older boys, ones who know my big brother, call our house and make obscene comments when I answer. Once my mother picks up the phone and starts to hand it to me, but I shake my head and back away. "May I ask who's calling?" my mother asks. "Oh, I'm sorry, my daughter isn't allowed to date yet." And hanging up, she smiles, pleased that I am so popular.

There is no one to turn to, but that's okay because I'm strong, I tell myself. I will my heart to harden. I would rather be seen as snotty than gullible, as arrogant than vulnerable. I don't need any help.

The moon is a silent, barren place, says a poster. The nights are bitterly cold and the days are unbearably hot.

A day on the moon lasts two weeks. An hour in science class also lasts two weeks. "Just ignore them," another girl says, but even when I do, the boys circle me, clutch their crotches, moan, and howl. I keep my face neutral. Like the moon, I will always show the same face, even when inside I am rotating and orbiting.

One of the boys snatches my glasses and everything blurs and the planets spin around me. My center crumbles, flimsy as the Styrofoam ball that was once Venus. Horrible things happen in the world, I think, but none of them has happened to me. Sticks and stones can break my bones, but these boys can't hurt me. They haven't done anything really, have they?

The wire and foil solar system above me says that the typical junior high student would weigh two tons on the sun.

I will always ever after weigh two tons.

Not long after, there's a sixth murder, a young woman named Nancy Fox. Nancy, like me. Her back window is smashed, her hands and feet bound with nylon stockings. Witnesses describe a man they saw in the area: white, about six feet tall, with blondish hair, driving a van with advertising on the side. For years, the newspaper has been printing composite sketches and descriptions of this mysterious killer: a guy in his twenties, slender with shoulder-length dark bushy hair; a guy in his thirties or forties, maybe paunchy with dark hair; now a young man, slim and blondish.

Someone sends a verse to the *Wichita Eagle*'s classified advertising department, beginning, "Shirleylocks, shirleylocks, wilt thou be mine . . ." An employee eventually recognizes this as a reference to the murder of Shirley Vian. Not long after, a letter arrives at a local TV station in which the writer takes credit for the string of murders since 1974. In it, he names himself the BTK Strangler and promises more murders. BTK stands for Bind, Torture, and Kill, which is what he does to his victims.

"After a thing like Fox," BTK writes in a letter to a local TV station, "I come home and go about life like anyone else."

I can't stop looking at the sketches and reading the articles. BTK could be anyone. Fat, thin, light-haired, dark-haired, in his twenties, thirties, forties. Anyone who goes about his life like anyone else.

Because he typically cuts people's telephone wires, whenever I'm home alone and nervous, I pick up the phone, seeking the reassurance of the dial tone.

In ninth grade, I'm an office proctor. I go to all of the classrooms and collect attendance slips. I have made new friends and things are not so bad, though when I step into all-male classrooms like boys' choir, an uproar ensues, whistles and heckling, while the teacher says, "Stop it, you guys," and laughs. Now, though, I can walk away and pretend that this doesn't still shake me up.

BTK will not resurface again for another eight years, and until then, his crimes fade in people's memories. Meanwhile, I learn more words that I didn't know. *Sexual harassment. Post-traumatic stress disorder.* I come to understand that what happened in science class was not my fault, and I wear shorts again instead of covering myself up with long pants even in the hottest weather. I eventually cut through my silence and learn to speak up in classes. I find good friends and dance in public even though I feel always tugged between forces, cycling with the moon while the earth spins beneath my feet.

Eventually, the universe will cease to seem quite so random. And many, many years later, when I'm in my forties, BTK will finally be caught. He's a church deacon, a Cub Scout leader, a parent, a seemingly ordinary person, and another mystery will finally be solved, reassuring me once again that for every question, there is an answer, and while sometimes that answer never reveals itself, it's there, waiting to be found.

But still I will struggle to tell my own story. People always want to know, "But were you raped?" As if only that most horrifying of violations would be enough to justify trauma. "But were you sexually assaulted?" And I won't know how to answer. Is being grabbed and groped and verbally assaulted a sexual assault? Even years later, in the age of #MeToo and #TimesUp, in an age of increasing social understanding that treating others as less than human can cause damage, there are those for whom only a rape or murder can validate trauma. There are those who still don't believe that a teenage girl has a right to be fearful of a naked man bursting into an apartment unless he's erect, unless rape is unambiguously imminent.

And so, for years I will go on wondering why I struggle so much with fear and shame and self-blame when, after all, nothing truly bad ever happened to me.

But for now, there is high school to finish. For years, I'll catch my reflection in store windows or mirrors, I'll examine photographs in which I appear, my heart pounding as I think, Please let me look normal, please let me look normal. Because deep down I'm afraid there's something hideously abnormal about me that attracted unwanted attention. Why else would those boys have singled me out?

In high school, I go to football games with friends. I think how normal it looks to be at the center of a lively group, laughing. But sometimes, I look beyond the inhuman roar of the crowd, beyond the eerily bright field and its unrecognizable heavily padded cartoonlike figures, some of them no doubt boys from my eighth-grade science class, to watch the moon making its slow way across the sky to tangle in the branches of a distant tree. On the moon, if you stand in sunlight with no protection, your blood will boil. But you will quickly freeze in the shadow of a large rock. On the moon, there is nowhere to go that is safe and habitable.

But I go on, a small speck on Earth, too mercifully unimportant to ever make the news. Please, please, please, I'll think when I hear a stair creak in the middle of the night or the thump of the heat turning on. I send out this frantic prayer to a god I have mixed feelings about, who I'm not entirely confident will protect me, as I pick up the phone and hear the reassurance of a dial tone. That sound connects me to wires that interlace over streets, that follow each other between poles, sagging a little, stretching on to safety, wires barbed by birds, undergirding the moon, underlining the stars, and holding the world in place.

Can This Marriage Be Saved? A Quiz

3. Think back to your early romantic relationships and the expectations you brought to them. Why did you first fall in love when you were young?

a. You joked with him in seventh-grade history class about how horrifyingly ugly you both found Hitler's mustache. Later you will see that as an awkward expression of your common budding passion for social justice.

b. A year later, you caught sight of him across the junior high cafeteria, head propped on elbows, looking sad. Something in him called out to your own sadness, but you also felt a surge of desire to protect him, to make him smile, to make him laugh again the way the two of you once laughed at Hitler's mustache.

c. By high school, after watching him for years, exchanging a few words here and there, catching his eye with the feeling that you were two outsiders who understood each other, you had decided that he was your one true always-meant-to-be love, the one you waited for like Penelope, biding your time, weaving and unweaving metaphorical shrouds. If only you could find the courage to talk to him, you thought.

d. You memorized "Annabel Lee" and whenever you passed him in the halls you thought, "My darling, my darling, my life and my bride." If only you could hold his hand, you thought.

e. After you read *Wuthering Heights*, you went around thinking, I am him. He's always, always in my mind, not as a pleasure, any more than I am always a pleasure to myself, but as my own being. But why was it taking him so long to kiss you?

f. Because it did take so long, to talk, hold hands, kiss, make out on his basement couch, stuffing leaking from the cushions like the tissue of a wounded animal. You went roller skating together, ate at Taco Bell, stopped at a diner for carrot cake after movies. And all that time you yearned for him, each small step the fulfillment of a long-held dream. You learned the pleasure of wanting. You learned how it could heighten the pleasure of getting.

g. He was so patient and understanding when you remembered the eight boys, and never rushed you.

h. He not only gave you his father's ring, but also a gold locket, a sweetheart locket, big and old-fashioned, carved with intricate designs. You were bowled over by the romance of this.

i. He thumped you warmly on the back, slapping a paper there, and you twisted around to peel off what you thought was a "kick me" sign. Instead, it said, "I love her."

FIRST LOVE: A CURRICULUM GUIDE
For students in Wichita, Kansas, 1976-1981

SEVENTH GRADE

History

TO LEARN ABOUT the feudal system, perform skits. You, a tall, skinny girl with long tangly hair, will play the strapping serf Bartholomew. A scrawny, bony-elbowed boy we'll call Cole is cast as your son John. He wears wire-framed glasses and his lips look perpetually puckered.

You're beginning to see that junior high is itself a kind of feudal system, except instead of a hungry peasant serving the lord and lady of the manor, you're a low-pecking-order girl who has come here from a small elementary school out in the country. Your homemade T-shirts with ribbing around the collar and sleeves, the yoked tops your mother sews, the blue work shirt your cousin embroidered and that you were so proud of, all are all wrong. Not to mention that you often have no idea what many of your classmates are talking about and wish a slang and curse word dictionary had been issued to get you up to speed.

So there you are, in front of the class, performing your skit, self-conscious, dressed all wrong, playing a serf named Bartholomew. You tower over your son John, and everyone snickers.

English

English class vocabulary lists accompany everything you read. *Deference, abyss, slake, hermaphrodite.* These are little use to you, not the words you really need definitions for, words that your classmates throw around. A *virgin* is someone unusually virtuous, you guess, because church Christmas pageants and readings of the Christmas story always refer to Jesus's mother as the Virgin Mary. You have no clue what historical concepts of virtue entail.

You are shocked to learn from your elementary school friend Stacey that a virgin is actually someone who hasn't had sex, that there is a word for that. You ask Stacey what *gay* means too. She has become more aloof, more concerned with being cool, since starting junior high. She says she is in love with an eighth grader. She stalks him in the halls. He leaves his top buttons undone so that everyone can see the hair on his chest, and she reports to you every glance he casts her, every expression on his face, every word he speaks to her. You thought you knew what love meant, but this isn't it. And you don't know what to make of the fact that every word you don't understand seems to have something to do with sex.

Art

Your first assignment is to draw something, anything, so that the teacher can assess your skills. Except your mind is blank. A girl at your table fleshes out a beach scene with playful dogs, bright-colored umbrellas, and guys in Speedos. Another outlines a circus clown and dumpy small elephants. You peel the paper off your crayon and sneak looks around the table. Kristie's people stretch out on lawn chairs in the sun, wearing dark sunglasses. Dana's elephant trunk curls around a peanut. She draws curves for the elephant's toenails and dark lines to suggest wrinkles.

Sweating profusely, desperate for an idea, you remember how, in sixth grade, you had to illustrate a scene from *A Wrinkle in Time*. You sketched a lumpy flying horse with Meg and Calvin balancing on its back. It was kind of a stupid picture, but you got into it, strokes loose and free, the unselfconscious way you drew back when you were little. You threw in stars and streaks of light. You had your limits—absolutely no rainbows and unicorns—but the picture still looked like something sappy by a little kid. Except the teachers loved it. They passed it around and praised it.

So now all you can think to do is try to reproduce your flying horse picture. You don't have any time and you're too tense. Your drawing looks stiff and silly.

The teacher halts abruptly in front of you, squinting and tilting his head. He studies you, puzzled. His gaze travels back and forth between the picture and your face. He looks amused.

You burn with humiliation.

Things don't improve as the year goes on. While working on a pen and ink drawing of a sagging cracked boot, you accidentally smear the ink with the heel of your hand. While cutting out a mat for another drawing, your knife slips and leaves jagged edges. The teacher often throws up his hands at your sloppy work and questionable taste.

He likes your rya rug design with somewhat phallic interlocking braids, but sighs when you choose red, pink, and white for it. Your room is pink, a color you have come to regret, and you think that a little red might toughen it up a little. It doesn't occur to you until later that your rug looks like a big Valentine.

History

You've never heard of Adolf Hitler until you find yourself in a small group trying to come up with a topic for a presentation. "I hate Hitler," says Cole, the boy with big lips who played your son John in the feudal system skit. "Let's do ours on Hitler."

You don't think Cole likes you, so you are extra nice to him, agreeing to his topic idea. Even though he's sometimes impatient with your tendency to cut up when he wants to be serious, you find yourself strangely drawn to him. You see him huddled in classroom doorways in the mornings, reading books, looking sad, and you laugh at his jokes during the history project and in return try to make him laugh in math class, where he sits across the aisle from you.

EIGHTH GRADE

Math

When you first enter the classroom, you automatically head toward Cole, but then you do a double take. He looks different; he has grown several inches and his lips fit him. He has grown into his lips. He is tall and tan with broad shoulders. His Izod shirt is skin-tight, outlining the swell of his biceps. Suddenly intimidated, you duck into a chair two rows away and three seats behind him. He doesn't turn his head to say hi.

Examining him, you see that he's not quite as tall and broad-shouldered as you thought, and his knit shirt is just too tight, not an Izod but a knockoff without a crocodile. His jeans have a worn sheen. Someone asks to borrow a pencil, and he smiles, braces glittering, and in that moment you see that he is your own weird scrawny sad Cole after all. But he still doesn't speak to you, and you regret that you didn't follow your first instinct and go sit beside him.

Then Stacey arrives, squealing: in the lunch line today, Paul said to her, "Can you hand me a fork?" She's pretty sure that means he likes her.

Math Again
This is the only class you have with Cole, and you find yourself living from one math class to the next, hoping to have a chance to talk to him. You can't stop thinking about him, about how great he looks when he wears blue, about how much nicer he is than the other boys, about how sad he looks sitting in classroom doorways before school, poring over books: *Zen and the Art of Motorcycle Maintenance*, *The Screwtape Letters*, novels by Herman Hesse. You notice the key on a chain around his neck. You can't stop thinking about the day in the cafeteria that he leveled his gaze at you. How your eyes hooked and steadied and all at once you were awash in inexplicable joy and deep tenderness and intense yearning.

And then, suddenly, in math, when he is only a few feet away and it's like all the little hairs on your arms are standing straight up, as if you are chilled by his very presence, you think, *I love Cole. I'm in love.*

You feel audacious. Brazen. Presumptuous. Like an imposter. How can this be love? When Stacey talks about love, about imagining running her fingers through Paul's tangle of chest hair, you picture fishy streams with hairy plants. When you think about Cole, it's like light glancing off a clear, cool spring.

English

Your teacher reads the *Odyssey* out loud. You imagine yourself as Penelope, steadfast in your love. You will wait for him, your true love, for twenty years if necessary. You don't wonder if Odysseus, so easily distracted by Calypso and Circe, is worth it.

The teacher's voice fades. Her head droops. The wine-dark sea laps away into gentle snoring. You drift out of your daydream to a class full of students shifting and exchanging uneasy glances while the teacher breathes peacefully, dreaming.

More Math

Math is effortless for Cole. People often scoot over beside him for help, and you wish you had the courage to do that too, but you're good enough at math that he'd probably see right through it. "I hate gym," you hear him tell someone, and your heart swells with love, because you hate gym too.

Sometimes you suspect that you are like a schizophrenic who believes that every swirl of wood grain is a secret message you must decode, every whisper of wind through trees a voice conveying profound truths only you can hear, the raised veins of a leaf a Braille fraught with meaning. You think of pioneer stories in which the gift of a candy cane or a penny in the toe of a stocking is a big deal. For you, even the most meager glances or words are treasures, things to savor. Even the smallest facial expression, comment, gesture, or article of clothing feels like a veiled signal to you.

NINTH GRADE

Math
Cole is not in your class.

English
Cole is not there either.

Music
It's girls' choir, but Cole isn't in the men's choir that meets next door at the same time. (That's what they call them at your school: girls and men.)

Gym
No Cole.

You bide your time. Plan paths from one class to another to maximize your chances of running into him. You feel stalled, still stuck here in junior high, waiting to move on to the high school, a ninth grader rather than a high school freshman like people in other parts of the country. Years later, you can't remember a single thing you learned in ninth grade, only the perpetual distraction of looking for Cole everywhere, wondering, sometimes, if he actually existed or if you just made him up.

TENTH GRADE

Gym
Finally you're at the big high school, so big you fear getting lost all the time, but the good news is, you and Cole are in the same gym class, taught by a young, doe-eyed teacher. An amazing thing happens. On the first day, just like that, as if you haven't been agonizing and plotting over how to get him to do this very thing, he comes over and sits by you, all casual, like it's no big deal. It is true that neither of you knows anyone else in the class, but

still, the moment that he plops down beside you on the bleachers seems fated. After that, you always sit together, you in your blue and white striped T-shirt and blue polyester shorts, Cole in his white undershirt and khaki shorts, and if you can still like each other in these unflattering outfits, it must be true love.

You're partners for tennis and archery. Every time you have to say the word "love" when announcing the tennis score, you feel your face blotch like a pink doily. You admire the sure flight of Cole's arrows next to the inebriated drift of their lazy companions shot by a row of classmates. Your own arrows tend to fall off the bow and plunk to the ground.

Waiting for your turn for tennis courts and the archery line, Cole tells you about his sister and his mother and his church and how he wants to be an Episcopal priest. When he says this, he quickly adds, "Episcopal priests can get married." He wants to marry you, you think, feeling your life fall into place.

Often while he talks, all other sounds fade: balls bouncing on pavement and smacking against rackets, traffic passing on the nearby street. You collect details about Cole. How he writes his sevens the European way, bisected by a line. How he says, "How bourgeois," when classmates talk about their cars and their weekend parties. How he pronounces the word "harass" like "harris" and says "I-ther" instead of "Ee-ther." How he likes a TV show called *Bosom Buddies* and has a German shepherd named Tequila and broke his arm when he was a kid, showing you the long scar, pink and shiny, inside his elbow. How when he sneezes, you bless him in Spanish and he thanks you in German.

You listen to Cole talk and you peel apart grass blades, reducing them to threads and tying the threads in knots.

With your thumbnail, you slit open the stems of dandelions, studying their milky innards. This is how you feel when you are with him: slit open, insides showing, pulled apart, tied in knots.

Journalism

You love this class, but the last fifteen minutes you're always distracted, watching the second hand on the wall clock, focused only on the moment when the tone will sound and you will fly out of your chair and down the hall, feeling like the embodiment of every patient, abiding woman in fairy tales, epic poems, and proverbs. You are Cinderella, about to be whisked away by the prince after years of drudgery. You are on your way to being the noble wife worth more than rubies, whose husband and children will rise and call you blessed.

Every day, Cole waits for you under a tree in dapples of sunlight, foil-wrapped bologna sandwich and apple spread out on the grass. When you arrive from buying your daily cheeseburger and fries in a white paper bag from a small, nameless joint across the street, he asks, "What took you so long?"

"I didn't take that long," you always answer.

Spanish

"Te quiero mucho," you learn to say in Spanish, because your teacher insists that's how to say "I love you." Since she is always wandering from her lessons to rant about the immorality of abortion and since "te quiero mucho" seems to you to actually translate to "I like you very much," you're suspicious. Is teaching you to say only "I like you" part of her militant campaign against teen romance that might lead to pregnancy that might lead to abortion? She is doing her part to prevent this, you're convinced, by only permitting you to declare friendly affection, not passion.

You look it up. *Querer*, you see, can also mean "want," and since your yearning for Cole feels infinite, now you're really not sure what your teacher is up to.

Geometry
In the margins of your notes, you scrawl your own proofs of Cole's love.

> *When I come to lunch every day, he asks what took me so long*
> *When it rarely takes more than ten minutes*
> *Which wouldn't seem so long if he weren't dying to see me*
> *So he must love me.*

Biology
Your scores soar during the genetics unit as you plot out the traits of your future children with Cole. High probability of brown eyes. Tall. Sensitive. Thoughtful. Attached earlobes. Straight hair. No dimples. Tongue-rolling possible. Right-handed likely.

But you're on edge, because Cole seems perfectly happy to see you only at school. Some of your friends have started going to Friday night football games, but Cole declines to come. And not just that: he refuses invitations to make pizza at Kent's, to go to see *The Producers* at the Marple Theater and stop by Julie's afterward for cookies, to go roller skating on Saturday night with the group of quirky friends who sit with the two of you at lunch. Why doesn't he want to spend more time with you? How will you get married and have brown-eyed, dark-haired children at this rate?

Gym
You've always hated gym, but suddenly, it's the best part of the day, along with lunch and passing periods, walking through the halls together though you've never kissed,

never held hands. Cole refuses invitations to social events, but once during passing period he agrees that after school he will come along with you and your friends on an excursion to a holography exhibit. There, standing behind you, he moors his hands on your shoulders in a very boyfriend-like way, so why won't he come to weekend parties, and why won't he hold your hand? Especially after he gives you his unexpected Christmas present, a sweetheart locket, though he does it in the most casual way, pulling it out of his locker during passing period. Still, your breath catches: Doesn't this mean he loves you?

In lulls between games and quizzes in gym class, you mention that maybe you'll become an Episcopalian, and Cole invites you to his church. He says he wants four kids someday, and you say you do too, and you agree that you like the idea of biblical names. Still, you never hold hands. You secretly wonder if you are repulsive.

One day you are walking through the hall together and a passing boy calls out, "Why don't you kiss her?" You roll your eyes, because while you are wondering the same thing, you have no interest in kissing in the halls in front of other people. Cole startles you by slamming his fist against a locker. "You don't know how hard things are for me," he tells you, and you're touched at how shy he is, how lacking in confidence.

JUNIOR YEAR

Algebra 2
You are always jiggling your foot, jiggling whole rows of chairs; you have too much pent-up energy to sit still. One day, Cole, sitting in front of you, abruptly reaches out and grabs your foot, stopping it, and the whole class bursts out laughing at this uncharacteristic gesture, a simultaneous

show of irritation and affection. "What's wrong?" he asks you one Friday when you're moping during class, and so you pass him a note: Why won't he ever agree to go out on weekends? Months ago, you accompanied him to his church one time and he was so excited about it that he made you a folder of Episcopal prayers, but he hasn't proffered any invitations since. But after you get upset with him, he finally, if often grudgingly, starts accepting invitations to go roller skating or come over with a group to watch *The Robe* on TV. You graduate to eating hard shell tacos on Friday nights while spinning around in plastic seats at Taco Tico, just the two of you, then going next door to the movie theater to see old movies like *Fiddler on the Roof* and *Jaws*. But you still never hold hands. He never puts his arm around you.

"Everyone holds hands," you finally say at the end of algebra, feeling inappropriately forward, positively brazen. "We should be original and just hold fingers." He laughs and agrees, and you do, hooking your little fingers together like a pinky swear, as he walks you to English. "My other fingers are feeling left out," you say at the end of the day, and by the next day, you have advanced to whole-hand contact.

Psychology
You learn about B. F. Skinner and operant conditioning, how a pigeon can be taught to peck a lever ten times for each morsel of food, how then instead of releasing the food at fixed intervals, discharging it at variable ones can encourage the bird to keep on pecking. By rewarding a behavior and then building on it, a mouse can be taught to run a maze, a child can be diverted from temper tantrums, a dog can learn to drive. Each goal can be met

by positively reinforcing each successive approximation toward it.

You break down your goal into steps. Talking, spending time together, holding hands: you've reached these. Next: first kiss, planning for the future, marriage. If you reward Cole for each small approximation, each tiny step in the right direction, you'll get there.

It never occurs to you that maybe it's he who is conditioning you, rewarding you at variable intervals, just enough to keep you hanging on.

American History

Waiting for your first kiss proves excruciating. After movies you sit in your driveway in Cole's mom's Dodge Dart, staring at each other and hinting around. "I hope your parents don't think we're doing anything immoral out here," Cole says, or "I wish I had more confidence. I wish I wasn't so shy. I wish I was normal." You stare at each other uncertainly for a while before you finally slide out of the car, cross the dark to the porch where flying bugs congregate around the light, hear him back out to the street, slowly, slowly, idling, a crunch of gravel, a rush backward, a puff of air. Will your hopes always disappear in a puff of air? You don't know whether to laugh or cry.

And then, finally, at the duck pond one night, you throw bread to the birds, who pluck it out of the air and snatch it out of the water. You talk and tear off pieces and throw them. You are so absorbed in the conversation, you're surprised to see that the bloated ducks have all drifted away and that the water's surface is thick with soaked bread, a layer of mushy pond scum. And you both laugh and then, because Cole is wearing a button that says "Kiss me, I speak German," you finally kiss him. For hours you kiss and talk, and he says in wonder, "I can't believe we're finally together." He tells you about how depressed he used to get, the way he used to plan how he'd kill himself, the way he'd light candles and get out a knife and just stare at them before he finally blotted out the candles and put the knife away. It makes you terribly sad to know that he'd ever been that depressed, but you've often felt depressed yourself, spending whole days in bed writing poems. All that is over now, you think. Now the two of you are together.

Now you sit close together during a class film. While a booming voice describes the pre-World War II climate in Europe, Cole reaches for your hand. Slowly, his index finger traces up your arm and down again, elbow to wrist, wrist to elbow. Shivers follow the path of his finger. It slips under your sleeves, toward forbidden territory under clothes. It brushes the white undersides of your upper arms, circles toward your bra strap, slides back down to the crook of your elbow.

Blood rushes to your face as your skin tingles with small glorious shocks. You lay your arm on his desk and settle your shoulder against his. The length of his arm presses against the length of yours.

Dust swims in the projector's fan of light. Occasionally, someone shifts, the curve of a shoulder or globe of a head nicking the corner of the film. Light and shadow jerk and jump onscreen, across Cole's face. His fingertips circle the bones of your wrist and map out branches of veins.

The film flicks off, and your ears ring in the sudden silence, your eyes dazzled by the shock of overhead lights. The projector's fan breathes quietly.

Everyone else shuffles and rustles and murmurs, but you can't move. Something you don't have a name for has just transformed you completely. If you try to grasp this joy and light and yearning, you suspect it will turn to liquid and run through your fingers.

"Let's go," Cole says to you, but all you can do is blink at him.

Extracurriculars

Cole is opposed to spirit week, pep rallies, football games or other athletic events, honor societies, clubs, or other school activities. He is opposed to anything that smacks of groupthink. Years later, when friends reminisce about proms and parties, you draw a blank. You will remember being completely happy, though, seeing Cole all day at school. Once it turns cold out, the two of you and all your friends eat lunch in front of a bank of lockers in D hall. You talk to him on the phone each night, and make out on a couch in his basement on Friday nights. His basement is unfinished, the couch mildewed, the bumpy walls water-streaked, his childhood train set spread out on a table complete with tiny fir trees and a post office. He puts clothes in the washer to drown out noise as you peel off each other's shirts and kiss on the couch with creaky springs. The spin cycle bumps to a stop. You hear the soft spray of water that introduces the rinse cycle. You offer him the little embroidered daisy attached to the middle of your bra, and he is scandalized.

This would all be perfect if Cole weren't less interested in making out than you are, if he didn't often plead exhaustion, a stomachache, a sinus headache. You attribute his pulling away to a difficult and distracting home life. His father died when he was five and his mother, who you've only met in passing, is pale and soft-spoken, haunting the house like a ghost. He tells you that she struggles with emphysema and mental illness.

You and Cole are on course, planning your future, even choosing a wedding date after college graduation. But more and more, he says things like, "I don't know if I really want to be a priest," or "Maybe I'll become a monk" or "When I graduate, I'm going to an underdeveloped country in Africa to teach," as if the two of you haven't already figured out your lives, how you'll go to college together, then move to New York City and put him through seminary by working for a magazine. There are days when Cole's mysterious sadness looms fierce and impenetrable next to your small, childish sorrows, and you don't know how to get through to him.

But then it's summer and you ride your moped to his house, the moped your dad got you so you could take summer classes at the university. You and Cole ride around together, pretending to be tough-talking, chain-smoking bad kids, sophisticated and European, not two honors students on a motorbike that only goes 30 mph. Cole tells you all about *The Confessions of St. Augustine* and religious holidays that you don't know about, like All Saints' Day. But in the midst of this, he says more and more things like, "I wish I had a normal family." "What's normal?" you answer. "I wish I were normal," he goes on. "I wish I had a normal life." You agree that you wish his family was more stable, but you've always felt abnormal yourself. Why can't you be abnormal together?

"You don't get it, you can't get it," he says mournfully.

Senior Year

Study Hall

"It concerns me to see a student of your caliber taking study hall," says the guidance counselor. You look at him blankly. You and Cole are taking study hall together so that your English and humanities classes will align. You have almost all the credits you need for graduation but would never consider finishing early because you want to be with Cole.

He is increasingly moody. He doesn't talk about it much, but you know that his mother has to be hospitalized regularly. Who wouldn't be anguished sometimes, given such circumstances? You feel like a silly, superficial child when he becomes distant, desperate to understand him, but he shuts you out and refuses to talk about it. Once, his mother goes into the hospital and he doesn't even tell you about it until the next week.

And then one night, on the phone, he starts to cry. He says he can't continue with this relationship. This makes no sense to you. After years of murkiness and uncertainty, the two of you have now been inseparable for two years, your life locked into a lucid picture like all the pieces of a jigsaw finally in place. How can he possibly disassemble all of this in just one night, one conversation? You don't believe him. He will come around, you think.

But in study hall the next day, he gives you a note. *Sometimes I doubt my sexuality*, he has written.

You wonder what that means. That he doesn't have any?

He asks you to return the note to him so he can burn it. In a world where you have literally never been exposed to the idea that love can take many different forms, where heterosexuality is so presumed to be the norm that you have no concept of any other option, it will be years before you understand his note. Instead, you will spend a good seven years agonizing, trying to figure out what you did wrong. It will be years before you get it, before you absolve yourself of blame, before you conceive of how deeply he must have feared more even than exposure or ridicule. How he might well have been afraid for his life.

English
During every quarter, you have chosen a module of novels to read, broadening your knowledge of Jewish writers, naturalists, and the Romantic period. You loved Malamud, Potok, Hardy, Dreiser. You read *Wuthering Heights* and "Annabel Lee" and found them to be more romantic than anything else from the Romantic period. Some, in fact, don't feel that romantic at all, and now you are having trouble concentrating on the unromantic Romance module. All you can think about is the way that Cole is avoiding you despite the dark circles under his eyes that suggest that he is miserable without you. You try to talk to him in study hall. "I'm not happy, and you're not happy," you say.

"I'm not happy," he acknowledges, and for the briefest second, hope flickers. Then he adds, "But I'm content."

You stay planted there before him, trying to process this, wondering how he has become such a stranger.

"Someone has to walk away," he tells you, impatiently. So you turn abruptly and leave, weaving between cafeteria tables, confused. After that you often spend study hall driving around town in the used car your dad just bought to replace the moped. You don't eat, don't sleep, and neither, it appears, does Cole, but his mind is firmly made up.

When you try to go back to the Romance module, you still can't concentrate, and so you're unprepared when, on the last day of school, your English final question is, "What does the arrow represent in Robert Louis Stevenson's *The*

Black Arrow?" You panic. You never got past the book's first page.

The seat in front of you, where Cole used to sit, is empty. He has been skipping classes. He even skipped the AP exam.

You try to concentrate. On the word *black*, on the word *arrow*. Black: like the last few months, feeling your way through darkness, the light on which you based your life suddenly erased. Arrow: you remember the confident flight of Cole's arrows during the gym class archery unit, how they soared like Type A birds bulleting south. How others' arrows wobbled and turned in flight, missing the target, how your own never quite rose into flight at all. It all seems like an omen, looking back, his sure sense of direction contrasted against your own waffling inability to make a future without him.

But you can't write any of this in an essay that's supposed to be about Robert Louis Stevenson.

Then the fire drill bell starts clanging, reverberating off the walls, and you put down your pen in relief and, with your classmates, scatter into the hall. "Has anyone read *The Black Arrow?*" you ask, whispering up and down the line, until you run into another girl doing the same thing, except she's asking, "Has anyone read *Anna Karenina?*"

You end up outside on the steps summarizing the plot of *Anna Karenina*, an act that earns you enough good karma that on your way back into the classroom, someone sidles up to you and says, "*The Black Arrow* is kind of a retelling of *Robin Hood*."

Back inside, you write, "In *The Black Arrow*, a retelling of *Robin Hood*, the black arrow is both symbolic and literal. There is a real arrow, which is black, that is an important device in taking from the rich and giving to the poor. It is also symbolic."

You know that you'll fool no one, but you go on writing. Later, you won't remember anything that you actually wrote, only that in that half hour you crossed the threshold beyond restraint into total abandon, because in the long run, what did this matter anyway? Maybe you wrote about how some arrows fly in straight paths to their targets. How others flounder. Maybe you worked in the phrase "slings and arrows of outrageous fortune." Maybe you wrote about the expression "straight arrow" and about stabbing others in the back with arrows. Maybe you pondered the origin of the word "quiver."

Years later you won't remember much about the paper, only that feeling that came over you, of detaching from your body and becoming immersed in something bigger than yourself, writing, writing, until you got to the last line, wrapping it up: "And so, in *The Black Arrow*, it is significant that the arrow is black, which reinforces the symbolism in this retelling of the Robin Hood story."

Economics

You didn't study for the economics final either. The first question asks you to explain the difference between causation and correlation and to give illustrations.

You're stumped. But then you remember how it felt earlier that day when you wrote your English essay, so you pick up your pen and get started, at first haltingly, then flowingly. Writing carries you back to that day in the sixth grade, before you'd ever met Cole, when you felt loose and free, drawing a picture of Meg and Calvin flying through the sky on a horse. You were so absorbed in your drawing that it hadn't mattered what anyone thought. You just drew, and felt more like yourself than ever before.

And so now you write whatever comes into your head until you imagine throwing in stars and streaks of light and rainbows and unicorns. It is soothing, this mishmash of thoughts and images that appear on the page, writing that won't make sense to anyone else but somehow brings you back to yourself, writing that you will remember fragments of even years later.

If you break up with your boyfriend after eating a peach, you write, you might conclude that the peach caused the breakup, when actually the peach is just correlated with it, which was caused by a million factors you will never understand. Maybe there's something wrong with you. Or maybe his mother is sick, maybe he feels burdened by responsibility. Maybe none of that has a single thing to do with the peach. Maybe it's not so daring to eat a peach even if it disturbs the universe. You read "Prufrock" in your college class last summer, and you're especially proud of that line. You're so proud of that line, you briefly forget your misery.

The last question asks for an example of a monopoly. You dash off one last line and turn in your test.

"God has a monopoly on butterflies," you have scribbled, and it seems like the most profound thing you've ever written.

Graduation
You and Cole march in together to "Pomp and Circumstance" because after your breakup, it was too late to change partners. You curse the mortarboards that make everyone look even more unattractive than gym uniforms do. But it probably wouldn't matter. Cole makes vague polite conversation with you, then keeps drifting away to talk animatedly to another boy. They crack up.

After graduation, you go home, not to any parties. You try to remember anything you learned in school beyond a few Spanish words and phrases, how to write a geometry proof, scattered facts about the feudal system and the Industrial Revolution, the concept of operant conditioning, which seems to work better on birds than on people. Vocabulary words like *deference, abyss, slake, hermaphrodite*.

You think of all of the words you still don't fully understand, the kinds of words that only take on meaning from experience, like *love*, or *sex*, or *gay*. You have fallen into an abyss. Into a thirst that can never be slaked. You wonder if you will ever understand.

Can This Marriage Be Saved? A Quiz

4. What went wrong in your first relationship?

a. You were young. Immature. Insecure. Possessive. Hurt when he didn't have time for you. Upset when he withdrew and didn't want to talk. Why couldn't you have been more patient with his moods, more understanding?

b. When he was five, he crawled into bed with his parents, and that night his father had a fatal heart attack. He'd always blamed himself.

c. His mother was dying of emphysema. A couple of times, she checked herself into a psychiatric unit.

d. Maybe one really bad thing had happened to you, but how could you possibly understand this? What did you know about death, physical deterioration, or mental illness? You once did a project on Carry A. Nation, who hacked up bars with axes. She had an ancestor who'd mistaken herself for a weathervane and climbed to the roof to sway in the wind. This is how you pictured craziness. Your first love's mother seemed pale and soft-spoken, thin and timid. She often called from her room in a quavery voice for her son to bring her Tylenol, a glass of water, a newspaper. You only met her briefly; she was so thin and angular, she seemed taller than she was, the bones in her face prominent, without softness. Maybe at night she turned into the hulking beast-like attic-bound Bertha in *Jane Eyre,* you imagined, rending wedding veils and setting fire to beds and lapsing into growling, straggle-haired incomprehensibility.

e. You just couldn't understand his pain, so much bigger than yours, although you would have gone on trying forever, no matter how fierce and impenetrable his anguish next to your own small, childish sorrows.

f. He seemed tortured and lost, retreating into agonized silences, emerging into anger at your hurt feelings, your tears. He told you he couldn't deal with so much and you too, and it seemed that something terrible inside of you had caught up with you again, that he had been pushed over the edge by the same awful thing that once drew to you eight groping, shouting boys in a biology lab room.

g. He said he didn't love you anymore while you piled the curls of phone cord onto your finger, mummifying it. He said this awful thing, and even then, he managed to sound like the one in pain.

h. All of the above. Why should there have been anything more? Wasn't all of that enough? How could you blame him for feeling demolished by his circumstances? Of course he had nothing left for you.

BEFORE AND AFTER

"MEET INTELLIGENT, SENSITIVE singles just like you!" the classified ad coaxed. I don't know if it was those words that first caught my eye or the advertisement below it, the diet pill ad that coupled Before and After photos. In the Before picture, a large, fuzzy woman avoided the camera. In the After version, a slim, focused woman smiled straight into the lens. The photos were supposed to be of the same person, but I couldn't find any resemblance between the two faces.

I was eighteen, driving my 1976 Hornet around singing songs about rain: "Raindrops Keep Fallin' on My Head," "Kathy's Song," and "Just When I Needed You Most," which had not too long ago played constantly on the radio: *You left in the rain without closing the door . . .*

I sang in my car, but in public, it was as if I'd taken a vow of silence. Talking was dangerous. I felt one word away from spilling over, losing it, falling apart. In the six months since Cole had abruptly dumped me, I'd imagined myself as the Before photo, blurred, sloppy, my boundaries slipping. I wanted to be the direct, confident, cleanly contained person in the After photo.

As if the pairing of the classified and the diet ads were deliberate and had something to do with each other, I sent in my ten dollars to meet other intelligent, sensitive singles. And that's how I, the girl who could barely speak, met a mute man.

He was a twenty-five-year-old accountant from Detroit whose vocal cords had been paralyzed by childhood encephalitis. I had once, in junior high, accepted the challenge of a teacher to remain silent for two hours. I communicated only by gestures, notes, sign language, and lip movements. I was disappointed that silence did not make me mysterious and intriguing. It annoyed my friends. They started ignoring me. Giving up speech, I saw, meant sacrificing presence and power.

It would be a long time before I understood that Cole had been struggling to admit to himself that he was gay, and so it still seemed to me that he'd broken up with me for no clear reason. I didn't get it, and I harbored a deep-down terror that something was so freakishly wrong with me that I would never find anyone else. It seemed impossible that I would ever experience again the nervous, breathless, giddy feeling I'd had around Cole. My confusion and grief were like a key turning, locking me into my silence. Who better to understand that, I thought, than a man who couldn't speak?

Getting to know someone through letters seemed perfect. I could usually say what I meant in writing, so much so that as a child I'd amassed sixteen pen pals in the U.S. and one from Trinidad. The ones who lasted included Helen from Minnesota, a good-hearted Norwegian girl whose father inseminated cows, and Jennifer from Pittsburgh, a lovely, well-bred girl who went to a private school and had a coming-out party. The pen pals who didn't last included those inquiring about the status of cowboy-Indian relations in Kansas and one who envisioned my native state as a beautiful, colorful place with roads of pure gold. I had to gently explain that she was confusing us with Oz, that we were the black and white parts, and no, Kansas was not actually a black and white state, but was in fact in full color.

"Sometimes I feel very far away from other people, as if separated by a huge barrier," George wrote to me.

"Sometimes I feel like that, too, even though I can speak," I wrote back.

I didn't know what to make of the heavy cologne that scented his letters or the cards that arrived weekly. At first, cartoon characters smiled on the covers, which opened up to humorous rhyming lines or jokes about friendship. The cards progressed to silhouetted figures strolling hand-in-hand down beaches and Susan Polis Schutz poems, then a field airbrushed with the pinpoint glimmers of fireflies. "You light up my life," the card said.

I had very stern literary standards, firmly eschewing what my high school creative writing teacher referred to as pimply weepy puppy-love poetry, sentimentality, and anything by Rod McKuen, a poet pictured on his book covers musing as he thoughtfully combed beaches or gazed out into the ocean. But if I was a snob, how would I ever meet anyone? I resolved to be touched by the effort behind George's regular cards.

"Why are you writing to someone so far away, and why did you choose me?" George wrote. "When I read your letters, I sense that you are a beautiful, vivacious girl that can have any guy you want. What are you looking for in life? A husband? A family of your own in the near future?"

What did I want? I wanted Cole back. I ran into him sometimes at the bookstore where he worked, and we'd inadvertently enrolled in the same freshman biology section. When he showed up, which was rare, he seemed sad. I wanted him.

But I dutifully wrote back to George, enclosing my senior pictures, assuring him that I was quite shy and far from beautiful, offering him, it turned out, the upper hand. After my admission of self-doubt, George's letters took on a lecturing tone and he frequently addressed me as "sweets."

Cole knew that I was allergic to cologne, that I was obsessed with the quirkiness of Emily Dickinson, and that I regarded myself as kind and compassionate but not sweet, a term I found diminishing. Sweet things were pleasant but had no nutritional value. I took myself more seriously than that. "She was old—so old—she had lived a hundred centuries and a thousand lives. She had loved beyond love, died beyond death," I'd written after Cole had abruptly exited my daily life. "Every worthwhile experience had escaped her or been hers—and all in the space of eighteen years." I was briefly swept away by the drama of it all. I was discovering literary distance. I could become a character, I could distract myself with language, and grief became less dire and overwhelming.

So it was, at first, with my letters to George, in which I could be beautiful and vivacious before I blew it with honesty and George turned condescending. Or maybe, I thought, I was just too quick to find fault. I had to give him a chance.

George sent a thick Polaroid photo of himself. The sleeves of his gray suit were too long, covering half his hands. His face was turned toward the camera, his body away from it, as if casting a glance back in the midst of retreat. But his legs appeared rigid, not really in motion, simply posing that way on purpose to obscure himself.

The real problem wasn't his seeming deception or his businessman blandness, though. It was that he looked nothing like Cole, who had long arms and staticky flyaway hair. Cole wore blue work shirts and heavy dark jeans and his grandfather's gold pocket watch and sometimes cowboy boots that made him even taller. But I had to stop making these comparisons, or I would never find anyone else.

Besides, George had an artistic side. He was an amateur photographer who took beautiful, colorful pictures of chrysanthemums and sunflowers, of tulips opening in the sun, of roses climbing trellises. He sent me 8 x 10s packaged in large envelopes with pieces of cardboard to keep them from bending. I framed them and hung them on my bedroom wall. I sent him some of my stories. "Your talent clearly ranges far and wide," he wrote back.

Speechless, we both spoke through our art, I thought. Wasn't that enough to have in common?

As my first semester of college unfolded, I started to make new friends, and I accepted a job on the student newspaper. I was starting to speak again, comfortable with the socially conservative, smart group of friends I met through the university honors program though often paralyzingly shy around the more nontraditional group of students, most older and married, who worked long hours in salaried positions at the newspaper. My life was changing, and my correspondence with George would probably have soon fizzled out, but he began hinting that we should arrange to meet. "I have a vacation coming up the first week in October," he wrote. "I haven't decided whether to go somewhere. Traveling isn't much fun unless you have someone to share your good times with. Maybe I'll come there to Wichita."

The idea made me uncomfortable, and I responded that I was pretty busy with school, and in addition to that there was no room for guests at my parents' house.

That was okay, he returned. I could just make him a reservation at a nearby hotel.

The only nearby hotel was a small, independently owned U-shaped building down the street from my house, next to a mobile home lot. Surely that would sound just too tacky for him.

That would be fine, George said, and with that, I felt stuck.

Fairly unenthusiastically, I informed my mother that this guy from Detroit was coming to meet me. My mother had made many cautionary speeches over the years about all the dangers that could befall a young woman. And yet when I announced that I was going to stow a stranger at a motel and entertain him for five days, she seemed oddly untroubled. She didn't ask why I had such obvious reservations, whether she could meet him, or if I was sure that our expectations matched. She didn't worry that he might be a serial killer. I wanted her to say no, tell me that it wasn't a good idea, try to talk me out of it, but she remained silent.

I assumed that George and I would just hang out in a friendly way, have some meals and visit some tourist attractions, and see if we liked each other. That's what I'd done last summer when I flew for the first time ever to meet my pen pal Helen in Minnesota, and she and I had had a great time. But somewhere in the back of my mind, I suspected that George might have a different idea of this visit. My suspicion made me so tense I refused to think about it.

As I drove to the airport, I entertained the thought of just not showing up. My life suddenly seemed just fine the way it was, and as I parked and headed into the airport, I worked myself into a state of nauseated dread and then panic. As they exited the plane, men appeared and searched the crowd. Their gazes settled on wives and girlfriends, a relief each time. Maybe George hadn't come. Maybe he'd stood me up. I was hopeful.

Then a slight man in a gray suit and striped tie, carrying a leather carry-on, strode briskly out of the tunnel and toward me. "George?" I said.

A staccato nod, then a head jerk, indicating that I should come with him. Hand on my back, he propelled me down the curved hallway. I hastened to keep up.

The cologne that had scented his letters was overpowering on his person. My gag reflex kicked in. I'd known that I might not be attracted to George, but I hadn't expected to be actively repelled.

I was too nervous to give him leeway for being nervous himself. His stiff, officious manner put me off, the way he guided me as if I were the visitor and he were the host. I'd known all along that this visit was a bad idea, but now it was fully apparent that this man wouldn't do as a stand-in for Cole, that I'd mistaken George for a reflection of some part of myself when in fact we were nothing alike.

"Did you have a good trip? Would you like to get something to eat? Is there any particular kind of food you'd like?" I asked before I realized that it was unfair to lob a volley of questions at a mute guy. At the luggage pickup, he scrawled a quick note on a half-sized white pad, perfect for writing one sentence at a time, then stared intently at the revolving suitcases. "Anywhere is fine. How about some romantic place where we can talk and get to know each other?"

Within seconds he had snatched up a suitcase and was rushing me toward the door. "Wichita looks like a cute town," he wrote as I headed away from the airport, toward the highway, trying not to sneeze now that I was in a closed car with his cologne. "Where should we stop to get to know each other?"

I bristled. Wichita might not be Detroit, but it wasn't a small town. "How about Long John Silver's?" I asked.

I had chosen carefully. No fancy, dimly lit restaurant: too much pressure, too hard to read his notes. Long John Silver's had bright lights and the food would arrive quickly, heading off awkward silences. The booths were more comfortable, the atmosphere less stark than, say, McDonald's or Burger King. Long John Silver's sent the right casual message without being completely tacky, I decided.

But when I suggested it, George leaned forward and peered incredulously into my face. I saw myself through his eyes, a sheltered eighteen-year-old in a long, plaid schoolgirl skirt who'd had the same boyfriend her whole life, who'd been completely happy with fast-food tacos for dinner, making out at the duck pond, late-night stops at Denny's for carrot cake. I'd never been to an elegant restaurant before a high-school journalism banquet where I had no idea which fork to use or the proper way to butter my bread. Last summer a friend's father had watched me wrestle with a thick juicy steak before finally demonstrating how to cut it along the grain. So far my first semester of college, new friends had introduced me to Chinese food and the bourbon-filled pastries at a French bakery. I was beginning to see how limited my experience had been.

As George set his lips tensely, making him look smug, I was convinced that he was sizing me up as naïve and gauche. Long John Silver's, the Carport Motel—what's next? his grim expression seemed to say.

I braked to a stop at the end of a long row of cars waiting to turn left. George knocked on the window to get my attention, then pointed to the other lane. It was clear.

Great, I thought. A mute backseat driver.

At Long John Silver's, George scribbled his order and fumbled for his wallet. I fished for my money, but he put up his hand and counted out the whole amount. Then he claimed a booth and began writing furiously. I collected our tray and took my time gathering straws and napkins.

Snatching up his fish platter, George pressed a note into my hand. I read it while I unwrapped my straw.

"I sense that you are lacking something in your life," he had written.

"I guess everyone lacks something," I said, annoyed. "How was your trip?" When I tried to poke the straw through the lid, the plastic refused to yield. I stabbed ineffectually. George grabbed the straw and shoved it through the slits. Then he bent over the paper, pen flying. "My trip was fine. Let's talk about you."

I didn't want to talk to a complete stranger about what was missing from my life. "Tomorrow I have classes, but maybe afterward we can do dinner and a movie," I said. "Is that okay?"

He nodded impatiently.

"And then Saturday, maybe we could go for a drive. You might like the Bartlett Arboretum for taking pictures," I went on.

"Why are you avoiding my question?" he wrote.

Maybe if I had to write everything I wanted to say, I too would be intolerant of small talk. But this wasn't how I wanted to define myself, as someone with something missing. And so I embraced the tyranny of being the only one with a voice. "I don't know about Sunday," I plunged on, ignoring George's loud sigh. "I could have gotten a free ticket to an Itzhak Perlman concert, but I'm not sure about two."

George suddenly looked alarmed. He flipped open his pad and wrote rapidly, "You should go even if you can't get me a ticket. How often do you have an opportunity like that in Wichita?"

I rolled my eyes. "I'll ask my friend Ty if she can get extras. She might be able to. She's practically perfect." It was an inside joke that slipped out, a line from *Mary Poppins* that Ty liked to quote, but George's face immediately darkened.

"No woman is perfect," he wrote. "Believe me, I've known many women, and they are all flawed."

"Well, no man is perfect, either," I said, taken aback.

"Some men come close," he wrote.

A chill ran through me. "So then I was thinking on Monday before class—" I began when I could speak again, but he put up a hand to stop me.

"I don't care what we do, sweetheart," he wrote. "I just want to spend time together."

Every note he wrote made me wince or outright flinch. This time, it was the endearment that, unearned, felt patronizing. I was going to have to steel myself a little better or he was going to think I had a weird twitch.

But I was bewildered. My high school best friend, my college best friend, my pen pal Helen, Cole—we'd talked a lot about logistics, trivia, plans, details, what we were going to do, where we were going to go, pet peeves, boring stuff, on the way to the interesting stuff: career goals, childhood memories, romantic dreams. Was this how relationships were conducted in the real world, this rush to intimacy? If so, I was hopelessly unsuited for romance.

On the way to the motel, George kept scooting across the seat, toward me. I cramped my arms against my sides, squeezing against the window.

"Well, I'll leave you to settle in," I dismissed him with fake cheer as I pulled up in front of his room. "I have to get up early, but I'll see you tomorrow night."

He hesitated, nodded, gripped his bags, hesitated again, leaned over, and kissed me on the cheek, his whiskers just barely scratching my skin. All the way home, I rubbed my cheek, trying to erase the feel of a stranger's lips.

My life seemed so normal the next day, classes in the morning, a sandwich in the honors program lounge. One more class, an afternoon copyediting at the student newspaper, a break with my boss to play Ms. Pac-Man at the student union. What had seemed so wrong with my life,

I wondered, dreading five o'clock and my surreal secret existence, the sham waiting for me at the Carport Motel.

I tapped gently on George's door, hoping he wouldn't hear, but he whipped it open right away and gestured me in. The TV was on—*Jeopardy!* With the curtains closed and the air conditioner pumping, the room felt like a cave, dark and chilly and musty and uninhabited, bed made tightly by a maid and undisturbed since, newspapers folded and piled on the table.

George gestured for me to sit. He peeled the wrap off the plastic cups, then unsnapped his suitcase and removed candles and a bottle of burgundy. After he'd lit the candles and poured the wine, he settled cross-legged on the bed and watched me.

I took a small sip and left the rest. Involuntarily, I perched on the edge of the chair, poised to rise quickly.

"Have you ever written to anyone before?" he scrawled.

"No," I said. "Have you?"

"Once. I almost married her."

"Yeah?" I tried to keep the incredulity out of my voice.

He moved over to the edge of the bed, his knees almost touching mine. I eased back in my chair.

His pen moved across the page. "We wrote for a year, and she planned to come meet me. If it worked out, we were going to get married right away."

"What happened?"

George leaned toward me. He smelled like wine and cologne. I scooted my chair back a little more. He turned back to his pad. "She was tragically killed in an accident. I keep all her letters in a box, tied together with a ribbon."

"That's awful," I said. For a second I allowed myself to see the terrible isolation of this man, but as he leaned toward me and I inched back until the chair was trapped against the wall, my panic took over.

"It's true," George wrote. "If I had love, I'd treat the lady like a princess. I'd buy her anything she wanted and protect her."

He waited expectantly for an answer, but it was so obvious to me that I had nothing to give him, I didn't know what to say. I was guiltily embarrassed that I hadn't acknowledged my lack of interest before he'd come all this way. I was appalled at how thoroughly I'd misunderstood what this visit would be, how naïve I'd been not to understand that George believed I'd tacitly agreed to sleep with him, fake romance, marry him, something. I stared at the floor, wordless.

All at once, he shifted his attention to *Jeopardy!* and barked out in a hoarse, odd voice, "Tower of London!"

"What is the Tower of London?" said the game show contestant, racking up three hundred points.

George looked pleased with himself. In a letter, he'd told me that sometimes when he was really comfortable, he could talk a little. I was so tense I thought I was going to throw up, and he was at ease enough to answer *Jeopardy!* questions?

"We should go," I said. My own voice came out a little hoarse and strangled.

Maybe George hadn't expected white tablecloths and candlelight; maybe he really only had wanted to spend time with me, or at least whoever he imagined I was, someone who wanted to be protected and treated like a princess. Though it was too late in the game, I took him to a nice restaurant where we sat at a table watching a flame flicker in front of us. He shoveled lasagna into his mouth, chewing with rabbit speed. I drew out each bite. His plate was clean before I'd finished half my spaghetti. He put his crumpled napkin on the table next to his plate and stared at mine. I chewed contemplatively, trying to kill time until the movie.

After a comedy where he'd laughed out loud at what I thought were dumb jokes, as we emerged into the parking lot, his arm flew out and landed around my waist with the efficiency of a carefully aimed horseshoe clanking against a nail. I hadn't seen this last-ditch effort coming. I stiffened. Yanking away seemed too mean, so we tottered to the car that way, ridiculous.

In the passenger's seat, he scribbled a note. "I don't know how to treat you," it said. "I don't know what you want."

"Treat me like anyone you're getting to know," I said.

He looked puzzled and defeated.

The previous spring, when Cole had said, "I don't love you anymore," I'd never wanted to move from my bed again. Instead I'd plunged into manic activity, resuming piano lessons after a long hiatus, producing essays for scholarship contests that paid for my entire college education, and joining Big Sisters, an organization that matched me with a nine-year-old African American girl with whom I spent Saturdays, taking her to children's theater productions and movies, teaching her to play jacks and sing camp songs, and visiting an amusement park. At the last minute, in despair at the idea of spending a whole day alone with George, I invited her along to the arboretum.

As we headed to pick Annette up, I told him about her. "I've been her Big Sister for a few months, but she really wants a black Big Sister," I said. Seeing my world through her eyes had been enlightening, the ways our activities reflected my own cultural heritage but were often a bit foreign to her; the fact that most of the actors in the productions we saw were white; the realization that, though I regarded my childhood home as modest, she was convinced that my family was rich.

"She's black?" he wrote. He looked startled, wrinkling his nose.

"What's wrong?" I asked as I swerved through the McDonald's drive-through for the coffee that he'd requested.

"They're just different from us," he wrote.

"Different how?" I handed him his coffee and a wad of napkins, days of suppressed anger surfacing. Now I had permission to dislike him, even to be outright mean. It was a good feeling to be poised on the brink of unleashing my full contempt.

"Sweetheart, when you see more of the world, you'll understand," he wrote. He took prim little sips of coffee and brushed a piece of lint from his pants.

More of the world? So I would think that Detroit was the center of it? So I could wear stinky cologne and call women *sweetheart* and think I was better than other people because I was white? And yet I remained incredulously silent, unable to violate the good-girl upbringing that made me polite even when affronted.

But passive aggression? I found myself unexpectedly good at that. I didn't bother to brake, rocking and jolting right over some railroad tracks. George sputtered and daubed at the coffee that sloshed onto his pants. At the next red light, he opened the door and set the cup on the street.

Now I was boiling. I wanted to make a U-turn and order him to pick up the cup. It was bad enough that he was

sexist and racist. But it pushed me over the edge to realize that he was also a litterbug.

From that moment on, I was merciless. I overlooked
nothing, forgave nothing. I talked only to Annette. She
and I sang every verse of "Found a Peanut" and "Three
Little Angels." George started to look pained, so I en-
couraged Annette to make up a few additional verses. I
relished having a voice as I followed my dad's directions
to Belle Plaine: straight south on Broadway, which turned
to 81, then a jog over to 31 right after Cicero.

An hour after leaving Wichita, I was lost in a maze of
highways and dirt roads and towns I'd never heard of:
Peck, Zyba, Millerton. I headed back east to Mulvane,
population 4,254. "Now *there's* a small town," I said. We
passed a sign for Udall, population 891. "Now *that* one's
really small," I said.

"Let's just go back," George wrote. "You're never going
to find it." He looked miserable, leaning forward tensely
as if to prevent wrinkling his suit, from my perspective
a lost cause. I'd cranked down all the windows, and dirt
clouded around the car as I swerved onto unpaved roads.

"I'll find it," I said cheerfully, accelerating, enjoying
the wind and the feeling of time passing as I sped along
toward George's departure in only two days. I leaned my
head out the window, breathing in the heaven of gas and
tar, escaping George's cologne.

Each of the first four times I left the car idling and
ran into gas stations to ask directions, George perked
up expectantly. But as I kept on stopping, he slumped in
the corner of his seat. Pretty soon, I was making stops
with cheerful abandon. I bought Cokes for Annette and
me. George just looked glum when I offered him one. I
pulled into a station so that Annette could go to the bathroom. I felt secretly gleeful that George, my prisoner, had

apparently surrendered all hope, weary and gray, sagging in a peculiarly rigid defeat against his seat.

"Told you I'd find it," I announced three hours after leaving Wichita, pulling triumphantly into the arboretum's gravel lot.

By then, none of us cared much about trees and flowers. George forked out admission fees and snapped a few obligatory photos, his camera clicking and whirring. Then he parked himself on a bench, arms folded, regularly flicking his wrist to glance at his watch. Annette and I sweated and waved away flies and dreamily persistent clouds of bugs as we read signs aloud: wisteria, sycamore, azalea, loblolly pine. We barely glanced at the vegetation they were affixed to. After a respectable interim and some complaints about the heat from Annette, who was obviously getting bored, we left. It took us forty minutes to get back home. I was surprised at how quickly we passed the sign for Wichita, population 298,000.

I'd resigned myself to another dinner with George, but he declined. "I have to pack," he wrote after we dropped off Annette. "I forgot to tell you the bad news. I have to leave tomorrow."

My spirits lifted. I didn't even think to ask if there was some kind of family emergency, or why he'd failed to mention his change of plans till now.

"Oh, that's too bad," I said. I was so giddy, it didn't occur to me to wonder how a man who couldn't talk had communicated with anyone back home or managed to change his plane ticket. All I knew was that I'd made a mute man so desperate to leave, he'd found a way. I had no remorse.

In books, in movies, people thrown together find common ground and learn to appreciate each other's humanity. George and I were just happy to be rid of each other, and it was years before I could appreciate the courage and unrealistic hope it must have taken him to fly by himself to meet a stranger. It was years before I let myself imagine, with amusement, the stories he told his friends and family about the weird girl he'd met in Wichita. When I let him off in front of his airline, George gave me a note: "Thank you for a very strange time. Keep in touch." I was so eager to go, I accelerated and the car leapt forward before I recalled that his luggage was in my trunk.

Driving home, I was filled with genuine, unencumbered joy for the first time since Cole had broken up with me. I'd thought that happiness required the fulfillment of desire—who knew it could result, instead, from overwhelming relief? I drove away from the airport, a little more aware of my own capacity for cruelty, a little less nice if still hesitant about speaking up, headed toward a million more mistakes, queasier than ever about leaving my sheltered world, but, at least briefly, utterly content. I was the woman in the After ad, shedding pounds with every mile. What did I want? George had asked me. I didn't know. But I knew what I didn't want, and there was something to be said for that.

Can This Marriage Be Saved? A Quiz

5. Why were you first drawn to your husband?

a. When you caught his intense dark eyes watching you across the college paper newsroom, you were sure he was a sincere person, above false compliments and calculating lines.

b. You were moved by those dark eyes and his stiff walk, suggesting some abnormality, like a visible manifestation of your own secret damage.

c. Walking across campus with him took forever. Everyone wanted to greet him, joke with him, query him for information, opinions, gossip.

d. He wore only natural fibers, baggy cotton pants and linen shirts, and only cooked from scratch, mixing his own pie crusts and ricotta manicotti filling. Next to your Betty Crocker cake mixes and poly-cotton blends, he seemed at once purer and more sophisticated.

e. One day, eating hamburgers in the shade of a wide-branched maple tree, he brushed a leaf from your hair. You were impressed by his ability to casually touch a friend without it meaning anything.

f. When you jiggled the Ms. Pac-Man joystick, gobbling dots and monsters, he rested his hands on your shoulders and you thought, How nice to touch your friends so easily without it meaning anything.

g. After the freight of your first relationship, of every gesture, word, and expression, you were relieved that there was no romantic undercurrent with him.

6. Which best describes your courtship?

a. When he made a bet with you and then maneuvered to make sure you won a free dinner, you thought, How nice to have a friend like this, with whom you could go out without any pressure.

b. He ordered red wine at a candlelit restaurant before taking you to an old movie at a refurbished downtown theater with deep velvet seats. And you thought, How nice of him to arrange such a fancy evening for a platonic friend, and then to insist on walking you to your door.

c. As you inserted your key into the lock, pivoting away from him to push open the door, a kiss apparently intended for your fast-moving lips landed on the side of your face.

d. You felt so sorry for him for misunderstanding your intentions, you patted his arm. Later, he said that's how he knew you were interested.

e. You felt guilty about your lack of romantic interest, and you acted even nicer to compensate for that guilt. So soon you found yourself with him at a Halloween party, dressed like a devil in cardboard horns and a red jumpsuit. Soon you found yourself in a car making out with your husband-to-be, who wore a nun costume. And although it all seemed pretty weird, as if your costumes were mocking your religious beliefs, when you caught glimpses of your chin or forehead in the rearview and sideview mirrors, your transparent self in the windows, you thought, That girl looks like a normal person, making out with a guy in a VW Bug with fake fur bucket seats.

f. As your future husband tossed his veil into the back seat, as he lifted himself to tug and straighten his habit, he held his back like it was plywood, a stiff, immobile board, and you asked him why. And he confessed to you about his disease. It had started when he was a teenager, he said. One morning, his legs just collapsed under him.

g. You were fourteen when eight boys cornered you in a class-room, and he was fifteen when his legs briefly gave out, and it seemed you had something in common, enough suffering between you to earn your first love's respect, to deepen you. As if that would somehow bring him back.

WITH ABANDON
A Courtship in Tom Swifties and Flowers

"I'm wearing my wedding ring," Tom said with abandon.
—Anonymous

"I am Mr. Bish," Tom said ambitiously.

"What's this?" asks Marc, my boss, managing editor for the student newspaper where I'm a copy editor, flipping through my notebook.

Marc is energetic and funny, scrappy and adventurous, with bright, curious eyes, and a quirky sense of humor. I knew from the moment I met him that we would be friends. Now I explain as he reads the list of quotations in my notebook: these are Tom Swifties, a fad a friend and I have kicked off in the honors program. Every day, people leave new ones on the chalkboard in our lounge. Marc's eyes light up. He thinks we should publish these as fillers in six-point type in the newspaper.

I've been desperately searching for things to laugh at since the breakup with Cole nearly a year ago. Most of last spring, I carted around books of Ogden Nash poems, cheered by verses like

Let the lovelorn lover cure insomnia
By murmuring AMOR VINCIT OMNIA.

Reading Willard Espy's *An Almanac of Words at Play*, I'd become fascinated by Tom Swifties, which had evolved from the series of Tom Swift books created by the Stratemeyer Syndicate in the early twentieth century. Their writers, using the pseudonym Victor Appleton, couldn't ever allow Tom to simply *say* anything. Every time he spoke, an adverb was affixed to the word *said* in order to helpfully convey his tone: *Tom said warmly, Tom said eagerly, Tom said happily, Tom said jokingly.* The parodies that arose spoofed this tendency by building in puns on verbs or adverbial words or phrases, as in, "'Judas, please don't kiss me. You know where this will lead to,' Jesus said crossly."

Sentences like that cracked me up during a period when it felt like I hadn't laughed in a very long time. Now, brainstorming Tom Swifties over lunch in the honors lounge every day with my friends, finding new ones scrawled on the chalkboard, and copying them to take to Marc over at the newspaper have become highlights of my days.

I'm a freshman who still lives at home, but Marc is older than I am and independent, back in school after a few years away, with his own apartment and a decent salary at the newspaper. I think of him as worldly, sophisticated. He has made a living as a carpenter, has spent a summer working on an offshore oil rig, had almost finished a degree in architecture before he dropped out of school due to illness. Now he's back, his major shifted to journalism. I'm flattered that he likes me so much. He's everybody's best friend; we can't walk across campus without being stopped constantly by people eager to talk to him. All of our coworkers think he's hilarious; he's always in the middle of a group of laughing people.

Secretly, I hope that Cole will see reason and want to get back together, but I'm happy to have this new friend to hang out with, completely platonically, I think, playing Ms. Pac-Man, Marc's addiction, at the student union. His pockets always jingle with the quarters he saves up for free moments.

"Why isn't she called Pac-Woman instead of Ms. Pac-Man?" I ask him. "Why does she turn around three times before she dies? It reminds me of a dog going to sleep." Marc laughs. Says, "Some people just don't think that much of women." Gives me a meaningful look: *I respect women*, it says. As we leave the union, he stops to buy a pink carnation from a student organization table. He presents it to me.

"I believe in shoveling the earth," Tom said prodigally.

I think of myself as very deep, unreachable. Since the breakup, I've been numb and silent. Sometimes talking seems like too much effort. But Marc is easy to talk to, and it's so easy to just go along with him. Sometimes I see Cole on campus. He is polite but distant.

I hang out a lot with Marc and his friend Kirk, who, like Marc, always makes me laugh. One day while I'm working on the honors program newsletter, for which I am editor, Marc and Kirk offer to help me fill a white space. They print a picture of bare trees outlined against a white sky and the caption, "Following a nuclear blast, the imprints of vaporized freshmen make a scenic design on the east wall of Hubbard Hall." The honors director condemns this as tasteless and insists I remove it.

Kirk is cute. He reminds me a little of Cole. But Marc has somehow claimed me, although I don't see why I can't be friends with both of them. Still, Kirk is always backing off, while Marc keeps making excuses to talk to me. He bets me a steak dinner that a newspaper story will print out to six-and-a-half column inches. I insist it will be six, and I win the bet. When I get off work, Marc follows me out into the shiny, drizzly dark. "Do you really want to have dinner?" he asks. He seems nervous. "I'll call you."

I like Marc. I like working at the newspaper. I like the respect I get from other staffers because Marc likes me. But I assume we're just friends. When he tries to kiss me after the dinner, I think, Oh. He *like* likes me.

The next day, he sends me a dozen white roses.

I start to have a recurring dream that I am pushing the same MDT command button over and over: "Delete anxiety."

"I am a Communist," Tom said readily.

Marc and I go to see 9:30 movies after he gets off work, new releases like *Chariots of Fire* and *Reds* and older ones in the campus film series like *M*A*S*H* and *The Deer Hunter*.

I sleep through many of these, since I get up at 5:30 every morning and have trouble staying up too late.

Marc finds me a little mysterious, and I know that he will never quite understand me, but maybe, I think, that's best. We're eating dinner at an Italian restaurant when a Bangles song starts playing. Marc says, "Oh, no, you're not going to like this." It's a cover of Simon and Garfunkel's "Hazy Shade of Winter." I do like it, actually, but I don't admit it; Marc is a purist, believing that bands who perform other people's music are by definition second-rate.

For his advanced reporting class, Marc is working on a story about a nearby convent, spending days shadowing and interviewing nuns. He is, he tells me, a lapsed Catholic, traumatized as a child by a nun who thought he'd played a practical joke on her by leaving a grape on her chair. He swears he was innocent, mortified when she made him sit on a grape in front of the whole class. It bothers me that he is no longer a believer. I can't imagine him ever attending church with me. Not that I really attend church anymore, but I imagine that someday, in my grown-up life, I will reinstitute this childhood ritual. I try to convince myself that it's promising that Marc still has a deep desire to understand and please the nuns. At least that's how I interpret his interest in writing about the convent.

We double date with coworkers, going to see *A Clockwork Orange*, a movie with rape and murder scenes that I find deeply disturbing. I am still shaken up when the lights come on. "Lighten up," says the other copy editor. Afterward, Marc keeps humming "Singin' in the Rain" under his breath and saying "Righty right" in a bad British accent. Everyone else thinks that he's funny. I smile so that they don't think I'm totally uptight, even though I secretly feel unsettled and vaguely ill.

Often I feel like the world has reversed, like I've become the Cole in the relationship and he is the Nancy. I am now the one with dark layers and inaccessible reaches. "Earth to Nancy," Marc is always saying as I stare out windows or off into space, lost in my own thoughts. Casually, he whips a bouquet of red tulips out from under his car seat and offers it to me.

"I took too many drugs," Tom said odiously.

After this Tom Swiftie appears in the newspaper, the advisor nixes using these as fillers anymore. Drug references in a student newspaper are inappropriate, he says. The fad in the honors lounge winds down, but sometimes I still find new ones on the chalkboard when I stop by, which I am doing less often since I'm spending more time at the newspaper and with Marc. Because Marc is into me, all of our coworkers seem to have decided that I must be interesting. Whenever I feel uneasy about my relationship with him, I remind myself how serious and quiet I'd become before I met him. I remind myself that he makes me laugh, and I need to laugh.

But I find myself laughing less when I'm with him, like after late movies, when he always wants me to come to his apartment. I do, and doze in his big brown Naugahyde chair while he heats water for tea and lights candles, the smell of a scorched wooden match hanging in the air for a second before being replaced by the candle's lavender scent. Marc squishes into the chair next to me. "This is awfully crowded," he says. "Maybe we should go lie down."

"I'll just sit on the ottoman," I reply. Marc's apartment is decorated in secondhand finds—a neon Budweiser sign, black-and-white postcards from the '20s and '30s, and funky tables originally intended for other uses—an old

Victrola, an antique sewing machine case. There's hardly anywhere to sit, but lots of things to look at.

Marc pressures me a little longer, but I refuse to lie down with him. Finally he gets mad at me and storms off to take a nap, clearly hoping to guilt me into joining him.

I sit and watch the candle burn and think about a poem I wrote in high school, comparing a softly glowing, steadily burning candle flame to my love for Cole. "Would you like to join the twentieth century, Nancy St. Vincent Millay?" asked my gruff creative writing teacher, who didn't seem to know that Edna St. Vincent Millay was an early twentieth-century poet, and who assigned the boy in front of me to rewrite my poem without the rhyme.

Recently, a mutual friend stopped me on campus to tell me that Cole's mother has a year to live. I remember how he used to say sometimes, with a hostility I didn't understand, "I can't cope with her erratic moods. I wish we could just put her in a nursing home." He'd run his hands through his hair with a fidgety guilt I'd become accustomed to. Now I'm the one who feels guilty, thinking about Cole while I'm on a date with Marc. I don't want to be here, in Marc's apartment. But I can't think of anywhere else I want to be except with Cole, and I can't be there.

Marc returns to argue with me about why I won't have sex. I refuse to give in. He finally huffs around, blowing out candles, and says, "Let's go." The flame I've been watching abruptly becomes a curling wisp of smoke. Marc pitches my coat at me. I remember how Cole always held it for me. We'd been proud when I mastered reaching my arms into the sleeves without looking. I know I should stop going out with Marc. I wonder, if I do, if everyone at the newspaper will stop speaking to me. I'm afraid I'll retreat back into my silence. Back to the bleakness of my post-Cole life.

I think about breaking up with Marc all night, until he shows up the next day with a bouquet of red chrysanthemums, his apology. I have no idea how I would break up with someone who keeps making these sweet gestures. It seems ungrateful. I would feel too guilty.

"How will I ever evade this prostitute?" Tom asked horridly.

At Christmas, after we've been going out less than two months, Marc brings me presents: a Pac-Man balloon and a pair of Pac-Man panties. I remember longingly the locket Cole gave me the first Christmas we were together. I've read that it's inappropriate for a man to give a woman lingerie unless the couple's relationship is intimate, but I'm also not sure if Pac-Man panties qualify as lingerie. I stuff them into the back of a drawer. The balloon, slowly deflating until Pac-Man turns hollow-cheeked, emaciated, hovers there as a constant uneasy reminder that a man has given me underwear for a present.

Later, in the spring, Marc trades his old car for a new Toyota truck, and everyone in the newsroom treats it as if it's a big surprise for me. I'm uneasy that he wants my approval about a major purchase, which seems to imply a greater entwining of our lives than I really want. And I have a sneaking suspicion that he dispensed with his car because the bucket seats inhibited make-out sessions.

Marc pressures me to help him replicate his mother's pregnancy April Fool joke, the way she kept planting hints that she was expecting without ever announcing it—prenatal vitamins, a crib in a box in the attic, the phone number of an obstetrician scrawled on a notepad. Word got around, and the neighbors threw her a shower. On

April 1, she sent telegrams to all her kids that said, "April Fool." The neighbors didn't get telegrams and thought she'd had an abortion; his brother's message somehow got lost and so he continued to wait for news of a new baby sibling.

This story makes me uneasy, but Marc's friends and family love it and make him tell it over and over. He wants me to cry a lot and drop a home pregnancy kit out of my purse. He wants to stage mysterious arguments and leave messages from an obstetrician in plain sight in the newsroom. He'll slip up with a comment about me eating for two, then clap a hand over his mouth. And on April Fool's Day, we'll have a big laugh.

"I don't think so," I say. The whole idea makes me uncomfortable, as if it's another way to trick me into having sex with him, or at least make people think that we're having sex.

But I feel guilty, like I owe him something, like the more resistant I feel, the more my debt to him increases. We go to see *To Fly!* at the Cosmosphere space museum in Hutchinson, and as we head home in the dark, still with that feeling of soaring above the earth, Marc stretches out an arm, gathering me to him to rest my head on his shoulder. "Love ya," he whispers, his breath moist and warm against my ear. I snap awake in a turmoil of confusion and obligation.

Marc tries to persuade me to come to his place, just for a while, but I just want to go home. The pressure about sex is nothing next to this new pressure. What if I can't say that I love him? Will his feelings be hurt? Will we have to break up? Will I spend the rest of my life alone? I can't imagine ever loving anyone else again, but I tell myself that maybe you love different people in different ways.

That maybe I will never feel again the kind of love I had for Cole, and that if I keep waiting for that, I will spend my life denying myself other opportunities, wishing for the impossible.

"Just for a while?" Marc says, and I realize he is still trying to convince me to come to his apartment.

"No," I say again. "I have to get up early tomorrow."

He sulks and my guilt multiplies. I feel bad that I don't feel the way he does. But isn't feeling bad a sign that I care about him? I do feel affection toward him. Isn't that a kind of love? Don't I sort of love him, on some level?

In my driveway, he jerks into park so abruptly that the truck leaps and shudders. I kiss his nose and he smiles grimly.

"I love you," I say before I hop out of the truck to the ground. I glance back at his surprised face, the smile that forms. I can see that I've made him happy.

I don't feel guilty. Of course I love him. He makes me laugh. He's curious and he'd do anything for me.

Except wait. I try not to think about that.

The next day, a florist delivers a dozen red roses to the newsroom.

"I believe in action words and words which denote existence," Tom said proverbially.

More than a year after Cole and I broke up, I still feel like I'm going through the motions every day, pretending to be a normal person instead of the withdrawn, tongue-tied girl I was when I met Marc, pretending to exist when often I feel like a shadow. I think that telling Marc that I love him will make him grateful and less demanding, but instead, our disagreements escalate. He believes that sex should automatically be part of a relationship. My belief that if you're in love you can wait seems comparatively silly and immature. I do not admit that I am hiding behind this belief, using it as an excuse to not have to face my lack of real physical attraction to Marc, or, I think, anyone but Cole.

"Kirk and I have decided that you're probably a tiger in bed," Marc tells me, and it bothers me that he's been discussing me with his friends in this way. I imagine myself with bared teeth, growling and clawing. I do not aspire to this.

"I want to marry you," Marc starts to say regularly. He seems desperate, wanting me however he can get me, mistaking that wanting as a desire for commitment. And in those moments, I see his motives with a detachment and clarity that will soon be muddied by my growing dependency. Often I wonder, Am I hurting him the way Cole hurt me?

But still I refuse sex, marriage, all of it. Until he blows up and says, "I don't know what the point of this relationship is," and storms out of the McDonald's where we've been eating lunch. And stops calling me. Leaves the newspaper for a job editing the yearbook.

I become a staff writer for the paper, covering a speech on Social Security at the Governor's Conference on Aging, a state budget cut that results in a loss of merit pay for civil service workers, a sunrise rally sponsored by the National Organization for Women the morning after the defeat of the Equal Rights Amendment. There, everyone joins hands and sings,

America, America, your daughters long to see,
That all thy good is peoplehood, from sea to shining sea.

I wish I could tell Marc about this. I know the word *peoplehood* would make him laugh, though I'm surprised to find how much I agree with the general sentiments expressed at the rally, because my family has always scoffed at feminists. I miss Marc, but not enough, I think. I miss the daily conversations. I miss the flowers that used to regularly appear on my desk. But that is not enough, I know.

"I write stories," said Nancy novelly.

My college best friend tells me that, in grade school, she read about how fireflies mate. "The males use their lights to send signals, and then the females respond, and that's how they find each other. I didn't understand how each male firefly managed to find the female that was meant for him," she says.

This captures how I've always thought too: that there's one person meant for me and that I found him when I was fourteen years old. But what do you do when the right person is no longer cooperating? My own parents didn't marry till they were thirty, but they never talk about previous boyfriends or girlfriends. The story is that they met in high school but it took them a few years to realize that they were right for each other. I've always pictured my dad pining away, waiting for my mother to figure it out. I've always assumed that neither of them ever even looked at anyone else. If I can just bide my time, surely Cole will realize that we too are meant to be.

Marc and I haven't talked for two weeks now, and the yearnings I sometimes feel seem disloyal to Cole—a longing to kiss Kirk, to run off with my Spanish professor. But I can't do either. Neither Kirk nor I would compromise our loyalty to Marc that way; my Spanish professor barely notices me even though I'm always trying to get his attention by being a little weird, a little offbeat. Like when he asks us to describe E.T., and everyone else uses *ser* and words for *brown* and *short* and *young,* and when he calls on me, I say, "Aparece una tortuga." Later I will learn that this actually means "A turtle appears," but Sr. Cardenas gets my meaning. Sort of.

"Una tortuga?" he asks me, squinting skeptically. "Una tortuga?" He sounds way too incredulous at the idea that E.T. might look like a turtle. I want to say, "He has a long neck, squatty little head, and bulgy eyes," but that is beyond my Spanish vocabulary. I'd like to be able to explain that E.T.'s appeal is his vulnerability, the way he resembles a turtlelike creature without any clothes or shell, without any protection at all. I look into Sr. C.'s beautiful dark eyes and know that he will never get me.

The weeks go by. I am lonely and I tell myself I am only attracted to these other guys because they remind me of Cole. One day I run into Marc.

"Call me sometime," he says.

"You're never home," I answer, which is true, but implies, I realize, that I have been making attempts. He lights up. With those words, I have sealed my fate. The next thing I know we're back together.

Looking back someday, I'll puzzle over this moment in which I give in, give up everything I think I want, return to a relationship that I know isn't right for me. Being with Marc feels, in that moment, so much easier than being alone. Having my future settled feels, in that moment, so much easier than uncertainty, than trying to master the whole dating thing, with all of its deceptions and expectations and hidden agendas. And I'm tired of resisting the direction my life seems to be pulling me. Marriage doesn't sound so bad. I imagine us going our separate ways during the day, then at night cooking and talking and reading quietly and companionably in the same room. I imagine a calm routine away from the turmoil of my current life. I imagine marriage as a refuge, like a soundproof room that will shut out all the noise in my head.

I tell Marc that I'll marry him. He buys me a ring, three-eighths of a carat that seems extravagant to me, a huge diamond set high in little brackets, flashing and sparkling as it catches the light. Too big, too high, not my style at all, but I'm touched that Marc is so eager to buy me something nice. Marc is calmer now. "I've decided that waiting to have sex till we're married is a challenge, like getting to the fourth maze of Ms. Pac-Man," he says.

"You know," Kirk says, massaging my shoulders one day in the yearbook office, "I wanted to ask you out last year, but Marc got there first." And I feel a little like territory in a land run, unavailable once Marc staked his claim. Kirk is funny, and has big hands and a big head and a big heart and once when he was drunk he laid his big head on my shoulder, and I'd liked that. Now, I try to focus on the things I don't like about Kirk so that I won't have these thoughts.

When Sr. C. sees my ring, he says to me, "Antes te que cases, mira lo que haces," which idiomatically means "look before you leap" but literally means, "Before you get married, look at what you do." Sr. C. says this to me often, and I get a little thrill. Once he even flirts with me at a Spanish class party.

But I am resigned to my fate. And Marc is so good to me. My friends and coworkers are always saying so, rhapsodizing about how romantic Marc is, how lucky I am that he's always bringing me flowers. My parents and friends seem to take our engagement as an inevitability, shrugging like they might as well not try to stop me if I'm determined to marry him anyway. I wish someone would just try. Would tell me this isn't such a good idea.

When my mom measures me for my wedding dress, Marc says, "You're almost perfect. 34-26-36. The perfect woman is 36-24-36." For my birthday, he makes me a cake shaped like a word processor and gives me red roses and has a T-shirt made that says, "'I write stories,' said Nancy novelly."

All my friends start calling me Nancy Novelly.

"See my pup-propelled sled?" Tom said dogmatically.

I am at Marc's mother's house, listening to Marc say on the phone again and again, "Dad passed away tonight. An aneurism." Nervous in the midst of crowds of mourners, I eat M&Ms out of the bowl on the TV until someone tells me that they are kept there for the dog, who does a trick in which she flips them off her nose and into her mouth.

I'm working to prove my mettle, standing by Marc during the days before and after the funeral, his mother wearing a blouse shimmering like water in sunlight, whipping up potato salad in her linen and silk and espadrilles, keeping busy, smoke wafting from an abandoned cigarette in a dish on the counter. The house filling with people, his mother fervently nodding her head, her whole body. The gin in her glass rocks back and forth until I'm afraid it will slosh out. Everyone's drunk by the end of the first night, everyone but Marc and me, and I wonder if it is better to shoot straight through the middle of suffering till you come out on the other end or to blunt the edges of grief, escaping it temporarily.

I send Cole a letter, telling him I'm engaged, and he calls to congratulate me. We go out to lunch. Out of habit, I look into his eyes. I think about Marc's eyes, intense, full of mischief and wide-open brightness. Cole's are comparatively dark and mysterious, concealing fathoms. I smile at him and he says, "What? Why did you laugh?" but I wasn't laughing, just falling into a habit of old familiarity. I tell him that I never meant to go out with Marc, that I actually thought Marc was gay when I first met him. Cole's eyes flick to my face. Then he changes the subject.

My best friend and I go to dinner the next day, and I tell her about my lunch with Cole. "It sounds like you're still in love with him," she says. Losing my appetite, I set my crumpled napkin on the table. The wad loosens, blooming there like a white flower.

"You draw circles poorly," criticized Tom roundly.

When Cole's mother dies, I want to rush to his side like I did when Marc lost his father, but I can't. Marc accompanies me to the funeral. We sit in the back of a sanctuary with exposed roof beams that have always made me feel like I'm in a luxurious barn. It smells more intensely of pine as rain pounds the roof, and I remember coming here with Cole, how he sat next to me, holding my hand. Today, on our way here, the wind lashed a loose telephone wire at Marc's truck.

When people saw me without Cole, they used to ask, "Where's your other half, where's your shadow?"

No one ever asks me those questions when they see me without Marc.

Cole and his sister and brothers follow the casket into the church. None of them looks at the crowd. People murmur sympathetically under their breaths at the sight of those four pale young people, now orphaned.

As I watch them, I think that soon I will walk down a similar aisle on my father's arm and marry the wrong person. Unless Cole wants me back. Maybe then things will come full circle.

Then I feel heartless. Am I really capable of going back to Cole without any regard for Marc's feelings?

Four men roll the casket to rest next to the altar, and Cole and his siblings take their places in the front row. I strain to see him, his stiff back and bowed head. His sister slides an arm around him. The building quivers in the wind. Water swishes under tires outside and blows in under the doors.

I remember studying existentialism in high school English. I am a free and responsible agent. I can shape my own life through acts of will. I will own the choices inside the accidents of fate that make up my life. I will choose the life that comes to me.

I will choose Marc, I think, feeling sad but noble.

After the funeral, I get into the receiving line, watching Cole accept with pained indifference handshakes, embraces, words of condolence. His sister's face twists and she rushes away from the line. Looking startled, Cole follows her. He opens the door of the funeral parlor limo for her, then turns, scanning the crowd, his gaze never lighting on me, before he also ducks into the car. In a garden alongside the wall, rain and wind have beaten and crushed yellow tulips, which sprawl flat on the ground.

"Whenever I race, I run off the designated path," Tom said distractedly.

Two days after Cole's mother's funeral, I drive under long, thick clouds, as if someone has plowed over the whole sky and left it in neat rows, a field of low-hanging clouds like unevenly stuffed, lumpy pillows. My heart thumps as I cross the threshold into the bookstore where Cole works to tell him what I wasn't able to say at the funeral. That I'm sorry.

"He was transferred to Kansas City," a clerk tells me. "He left the day after his mother's funeral."

Under the ravaged sky, the bulky, wind-pushed clouds, my last hopes derailed, I drive home.

The days disappear, eaten away like the dots in Ms. Pac-Man. Soon I am walking down the aisle on my dad's arm, flashes going off in my eyes, while Marc scans the crowd, grinning. When I reach the altar, he takes my hand the way the minister has instructed him. I vow to love and honor him. I have made a point about striking the word *obey*, and I've requested that the minister not introduce us at the end of the ceremony as *Mr. and Mrs. Marc*, but as *Marc and Nancy*. I didn't want to change my name, but his mother frowned when I said so, and that's all it had taken for me to capitulate. Marc promises to love and honor me. He slides a gold band onto my finger, next to my engagement ring. And then comes the solo, the unity candle, the minister's introduction.

"I now present Mr. and Mrs. Marc—" He stops. "Marc and Nancy—" Our guests laugh. And Marc and I scurry out of the sanctuary in an undignified recessional, laughing with relief. Many years later, I'll be stricken by that reaction of my younger self: not joy, not happy anticipation of our future, but relief that I've managed to get myself married, and now I don't have to agonize anymore over whether it's the right decision. It's done, and there's no turning back.

As I pose for pictures with Marc, my bridesmaids, his family, my family, my dad says, "Remember when you were a little girl and you always ran away from the camera? You were a blur in every picture I took."

I don't run away now, although I am surprised to see the pictures later, that I am not a blur. Because it feels like the clear lines of who I am have smeared, like I am nebulous, formless, without definition, without borders or boundaries, twenty years old, a wife.

"I have no flowers," Tom said lackadaisically.

At the end of the reception, I toss backward my bouquet of cream-colored roses and ivory calla lilies scattered with baby's breath. The church's basement has a low ceiling. The bouquet hits it and bounces to the floor.

We all stare at it for a startled second.

I retrieve it and throw it again.

Can This Marriage Be Saved? A Quiz

7. What made you decide to marry him?

a. You don't know, considering that you felt no jealousy, grief, or regret when your distance led him to sleep with an old girlfriend.

b. Because he proposed while the two of you sat in the window of his apartment and bells tolled from a nearby church. The bells lent portent to that moment, made it seem less like your life than a life from a story. Still, you said no.

c. When you said no, he promised anything, whatever you wanted—four children with biblical names, like you and your first love had planned, a career change, a religious conversion, regular church attendance. But when you still said no, and he sulked in the kitchen, you curled up in a Naugahyde chair in a circle of lamplight. You pretended his cozy attic apartment was yours, there above the streetlights as they popped on at dusk.

d. You were haunted by a terrible guilt that you didn't feel the way he wanted you to. You were socialized to believe that the worst things a woman could do was have an opinion, take up space, or hurt others' feelings. You were socialized to believe that it was not okay to say no. And so, slowly, you caved.

e. He bought you a ring, a diamond too big, set too high, twinkling on your finger like a distant star, snagging on clothes and furniture. When you wore it, you felt like a different person, and you thought, *I could be this person, this simpler, happier person than the one I really am.*

f. When his father died, he needed you. When you left together for the Rosary, sunlight flooded the trees. When you returned, each leaf curved, cradling the remaining light. First the light had held the leaves. Now the leaves held the light.

g. Together you kicked the frothy heads off dandelions until the air swam with seeds, and you talked about the future. And back inside, his mother's front hall was tiled with mirrors, so that a multiplicity of identical mourners kept coming and going. You thought, somewhat inaccurately, that these were people who weren't afraid to see themselves.

h. When your first love's mother died, he called to tell you and you didn't recognize his voice.

i. Your first impulse was still to rush to his side, but instead your husband-to-be was the one who sat beside you in your first love's church. Outside, wind whined and raindrops splattered.

j. You could bear your life if you thought of it as a story: bells tolling in a window, rain on the day of a funeral, slashing across car windows and blowing ethereally over the road. Church doors rattling and trembling, wind slapping rain under them, leaving puddles on the floor.

k. When your solemn and pale first love followed behind the shiny oak casket as it was wheeled up the aisle, you thought about how you would soon walk up another aisle to marry the wrong person. How right now you were in the wrong place, way in the back of the church, with the wrong person, and it seemed there was nothing you could do about it.

l. But still you inched toward your first love in the receiving line, imagining the strength of his hand clasping yours, your diamond biting into his palm, your breasts crushed between you in a hug. You imagined these brief touches awakening his desire. But when you were steps away from him, he whirled around and pushed out the side door. You surged after him with the rest of the confused crowd. He turned. He scanned faces with a gaze that never lit on you. He ducked into the funeral parlor limo, disappearing behind dark windows. Puddles rippled in the wind. The wind broke the stems of tulips and left them flattened along the walk.

m. The next day, he moved away, leaving no forwarding address.

HONEYMOON RESERVATIONS

AT THE END of every church service when I was a child, the congregation crooned,

> Softly and tenderly Jesus is calling,
> Calling for you and for me ...

It took all of my will to resist the gravitational pull of the backward-sloping bench, sitting forward as I fisted my hands over the rounded pew-back in front of me and held myself stiff. My family, who occupied the back row, never sang or swayed or tapped a finger or jiggled a foot in time to the music. Any fidgeting that had gone on during the sermon abruptly halted as we sat, impervious, attempting to appear unmoved by the haunting chords.

> Why should we tarry when Jesus is calling?
> Calling, oh, sinner, come home,

everyone else sang, and here and there someone popped up, slipping out of pews to make or renew confessions of faith. I stayed rooted to the back row with my unsmiling, unsinging family, trying to look bored and nonchalant in the face of those gently seductive voices:

Come home, come home
Ye who are weary come ho-o-ome ...

Soon the hymn would end and my family would tiptoe out, too shy to mingle, exiting through side doors to avoid handshakes and small talk, and all the way home my brothers and I would argue over who was taking up more than their fair share of space in the back seat. The mood left by the hymn's mournful chorus was dispelled, and until the next week I'd forget how, as voices swelled on that three-syllable *home*, they curled over me like waves pulling me out to sea, they tugged like an undertow of longing in my heart, they washed over me like a reassurance that however adrift I might be, some comforting shore awaited me, some place I belonged.

I forgot until the next Sunday, when that hymn would once again invite me to come home, come home, and in those moments, my life seemed to unfold before me: I would grow up and get a job and fall in love and marry and have children and a career. I could belong to such a life so simply and naturally, if I could just hang onto my belief, watching my life proceed according to His perfect plan.

I made my own confession of faith at the age of twelve, afraid that I'd better go for it now lest my resolve weaken later. So I repeated after the minister, "I believe that Jesus Christ is the son of the living God ..." and two weeks later, on Mother's Day, I wore a white choir gown down the steps to the baptismal font. The minister said, "I baptize you in the name of the Father and the Son and the Holy Spirit," and then the water closed over my head. In the minister's strong grip, I came up, robe clinging, long hair streaming.

Photos from later that day show me in a short purple dress, squinting and smiling in front of the garage. I remember feeling not so much new or cleansed as relieved at having secured my salvation for some older, more skeptical self who had just narrowly escaped eternal damnation thanks to my foresight on her behalf.

In snapshots from eight years later, I am at home posing in my ivory wedding dress and knee socks during a fitting, and then, the day of the wedding, skinny and barefoot in the same dress, waiting for my maid of honor to fetch some hose. My normally wavy, light hair professionally tamed for the occasion, I laugh toward my husband-to-be. He shows off his high-top tennis shoes, dyed black to match his tuxedo.

More photos, long since lost: In her silk dress and motionless perm, my mother-in-law smiles stiffly at her son's impropriety. My parents and brothers and I pose, *American Gothic* rigid in formal clothes. Marc and I stand before one hundred guests, flanked by bridesmaids and groomsmen, my veil pulled back, Marc's pants hiked up a little to make sure everyone can see his shoes.

What the pictures don't show is the tears in my eyes as the soloist's first notes struck up. Marc had threatened to request "The Thrill Is Gone" but surprised me instead with Bob Dylan's "Never Say Goodbye." When I surreptitiously lifted the sleeve of my wedding dress, my runny nose met only scratchy lace. Hand in Marc's, I swung his arm up to swipe my nose with the velvety sleeve of his rented tux. My maid of honor snickered.

I will, I said, and my marriage began.

The snapshots seem to finish off the story: framed by the truck window, hair speckled with birdseed thrown in lieu of rice, Marc and I wave and laugh as we pull away from the curb, like any other couple heading off to our happily ever after. There is no sign in my smile once again of the relief I felt, this time at having gotten myself married before I changed my mind, another favor I did for an older self who might lose her chance.

Halfway to Harper, Kansas, our honeymoon destination, my new husband cracked the driver's window of his Toyota truck and sighed with contentment.

I tensed, steeling myself to say the right thing if he told me he loved me or asked if I was happy. Warm air blew through the cab, lifting tufts of his thinning hair. To my relief, Marc didn't speak after all. He just hummed under his breath in his tuneless tone-deaf way and kept steering one-handed as if the road were the furthest thing from his mind.

I was twenty years old and didn't remember living anywhere but the house where I'd grown up. I kept thinking about the echoing rooms of our new duplex with clean white walls and light neutral carpet, my boxes of books stacked in the basement, my clothes huddled together on hangers in a cavernous bedroom closet. I kept remembering how, after the ceremony in my childhood church and before the reception at my childhood home, I'd slipped into my childhood bedroom to struggle free of my wedding gown.

My little brother had already started obliterating my presence. A pyramid of brown plaid wallpaper rolls had been assembled to cover my rose-and-trellis pattern. I'd chosen it when I was twelve for its old-fashioned quaintness, like something out of one of my favorite girls' novels. Now, heavy-metal albums leaned against the corner stereo where my Simon and Garfunkel and musical soundtracks had been. My brother's test of the quality of music had to do with its power to cause car windows to collapse and dishes to leap off of shelves. Ripped from its track when he had slapped on tape, the closet door now hung askew and was plastered with posters of bands with spiky hair and bared teeth. The room smelled vaguely of cedar chips and hamster urine; the wheel in the corner creaked under the hamster's feet. I couldn't understand how my brother could reconcile his love for small animals with his passion for bands that bit the heads off them.

Standing alone in that room, scratchy lace and satin dress pooled at my feet, the rumble of voices downstairs and the doorbell's frequent interjections, doors slamming, more footsteps, I had fought the onset of the desolation that had since gaped wider with every passing hour. Now, in the quiet of truck tires sighing against the road, I felt as if I might fall into that trench and never climb out.

Marc reached out to comb his fingers through my hair, a husbandly gesture, affectionate and proprietary. Darkness pressed in on the truck and my whole life was in boxes, my life was a box. I fixed my eyes on the moon, just a sliver like a glimmer of a frown, like an inadequate low-walled cup, a moon that my uncles would say didn't hold water. It held nothing; partial, downturned, it spilled out stars and darkness and memory.

I shut my eyes, a child again in the back seat of a powder blue Impala that glided silent as a spaceship down long highways, followed by the bright moon above. I was six, seven, eight, and not long before, a man had landed on that moon. My dad took blurred black-and-white photos of the black-and-white TV the day the Apollo 11 made its wobbly landing, the day the first man took his first small step. The bubble seat covers molded craters in my cheeks as I thought about a picture book on my shelf at home, *Someday You Will Go to the Moon*, starring a blond boy who went on vacation to the colonized moon.

I didn't dream of romance, that young. I dreamed instead of the friends I would find someday, people who felt as much like aliens in this world as I did. I dreamed of a wide-open future and my own giant leaps for mankind.

From the front seat the voices of my parents sounded as if they were transmitted from another planet. Someday, I used to think, drowsy and secure. Someday I will go to the moon.

"Don't bite your fingernails," said a voice close to my ear and I opened my eyes, twenty years old and on the way to my honeymoon. I had managed to bite and tear most of my nails to the quick in the last few hours; now I caught the last one in my teeth and ripped it off. Up in the sky hung that faint curve of moon. In my palm lay the curved sliver of fingernail.

"Look," I said to Marc. "I'm in parentheses."

He ruffled my hair. "You're so weird," he said.

As soon as I entered our room at Rosalea's Hotel, a tulip-red building in downtown Harper, I burst into tears.

"I'm just happy," I assured Marc as I gazed around in horror.

I'd imagined an elegant suite—thick carpets, scented candles, fresh flowers. The walls of this room were papered in silver and gold foil that reflected the light. Mannequin arms and torsos lounged on top of the couch and dresser and in the middle of the canopy bed.

Gingerly I pushed aside a plastic leg and sank onto the vinyl fainting couch, examining the room's centerpiece, a sandbox table. Magazine pictures of Lily Tomlin had been glued to Popsicle sticks and stuck in the sand of this homemade shrine. A whole choir of Lily Tomlins smiled slyly at me.

"Did you tell them that it was our honeymoon?" I sobbed.

"It's the Lily Tomlin Shrine Room." Marc sounded crushed. "We were on the waiting list. I thought it would be fun." He hastened around the room in search of Kleenex and returned looking slightly desperate. "I guess it's not very romantic," he said, "but feel what good quality this toilet paper is."

I blew my nose and attempted a smile.

Marc squatted beside me, dark eyes expectant. "Let's go to bed," he said.

I'd been too busy and nervous to eat earlier. Dizzy, I closed my eyes. White walls rose before them, the strange apartment that contained my whole boxed-up past, white swirling like snow covering the field across the street from where I used to wait for the school bus, air glittering, snowflakes caught there like whirling dust in motes of sunlight, and the field stretching white, sun leaping, glinting, glimmering, panicking my snow-blind eyes.

"Are you okay?" Marc's anxious face hovered above me and I felt like some stereotype of a fragile woman about to faint on my wedding night.

"I should have eaten," I said.

"There's some wedding mints in the glove compartment."

I made a face. "Remember that hamburger place we passed on the way in? Please? I'm starved." It scared me that I could become this girl who shamelessly wheedled, a tone I knew Marc couldn't resist.

I'd thought that when the time came, some wifely instinct would kick in and sleeping with Marc wouldn't seem so bad. Instead, all that kicked in was a dread so heavy with doom, my whole future felt blighted, concentrated in that one reality: I was going to have to sleep with Marc.

I told myself that I had no right to feel so repelled. Marc was a nice person, and my friends thought he was cute. And since no one else had ever picked up on my reservations, maybe it was normal to feel this way, maybe it was just nerves, maybe all brides felt this way. The minister who'd married us had seen no reason to be concerned; in fact, because Marc was twenty-eight to my twenty, the minister had scrapped the required counseling sessions. "You're an older couple," he said by way of explanation.

My parents and friends had only responded with bland pleasantries when I'd decided to marry Marc. I felt oddly abandoned—why didn't anyone express any concern? But if they had, would I have admitted to the mistake I was making? Wasn't it shallow to long for Cole's tall, thin build, his fine cowlicky hair, his long arms? It felt wrong when Marc embraced me. I'd known him two years, but I still felt like I was forcing intimacy with a stranger.

Marc's departure to get me a hamburger skimmed off the top of my despair. I gathered my overnight bag and a towel from the bathroom, which had a claw-footed, gold-spouted tub but no shower. The shower room was at the end of the hall—the Jesus Shower Room, said a sign on the door.

There, I promptly fell apart again. Jesuses surrounded me: a laminated watercolor of Jesus on the cross, head drooping; a slick magazine picture in a plastic frame of Jesus herding sheep; a slightly warped wooden plaque of a praying Jesus on his knees; a red velvet Jesus, hands raised to reveal puncture wounds dripping red velvet blood.

Stock-still among all of those bearded, wounded Jesuses, I fully understood that I had crossed into an alien new life.

Retreating behind the shower's Plexiglas door, I turned the knob that unleashed a spray of hot water. I closed my eyes as more tears leaked out. Miles away, boxes of photo albums, vacation souvenirs, childhood dolls and stuffed animals, my whole history and identity, towered in the middle of a strange living room. I thought about how the four milestones of a woman's life were birth, marriage, childbirth, and death, and how, at twenty, I was already halfway done.

As water poured over me, I cried over my meager belongings in precarious and temporary positions, my life that was almost half over, my first love who had failed to execute the sort of dramatic rescue at the altar I'd fantasized about but never really believed in. I cried at the way, during the reception, Marc and his friends had gone across the street to drink champagne because my mother wouldn't allow it in the house; the way when Marc kissed me afterward, he'd tasted dangerous and forbidden. I mourned my lost safety, my new nightmarish life, and the way the mocking arrangement of pictures of Jesus blurred by my tears and the water-streaked shower door signified the loss of all goodness, truth, and reverence.

The hamburger was cold and rubbery by the time I got back to the room, but I wolfed it down anyway and wished I dared ask Marc to go after another one. He was nearly asleep, though, so I unwound the towel, shrugged on my cotton nightgown, and crawled into the waterbed.

At least it was over quickly: my first knowledge that there was a fine line between pain and pleasure, and I had fallen on the wrong side. Marc went right to sleep, but I lay awake picturing the ivory gown in which I'd said my vows, a gown previously worn by my mother and two aunts who had had long, apparently happy marriages. I tossed and turned under the sheet that felt as heavy as the responsibility of that dress. Would anyone forgive me if my marriage ended and I ruined the dress's symbolism? I could only remember two divorces ever in the history of my family, both due to the flights of unfaithful wives who left behind my steady uncles and their young children. One uncle was too embarrassed to announce the dissolution of his marriage. He just started showing up alone at gatherings, and after about five years, we all figured it out.

Marc stirred and snuggled up closer to me. I lay awake worrying and hoping I would grow to like the feel of his breath on my hair.

Sometimes, when I look back now as if from another lifetime, I am mystified: Why did I marry someone with whom I wasn't in love, to whom I wasn't attracted, for whom I felt mostly a fraternal affection? Marc was a good person, I thought when he begged me to marry him. Someone in the world ought to get what he wanted.

"Let's get married," I'd said, planning to stall sex till after the wedding, when by force of will I expected to be attracted to him.

The morning after the wedding when I woke in the Lily Tomlin Shrine Room at Rosalea's Hotel in Harper, Kansas, the gold band on my finger surprised me. The day before seemed like a dream, all the professionally wrapped gifts in shiny white paper, the little net bags of birdseed, the powder blue napkins with our names and the date stamped in silver foil.

As I eased out of the path of Marc's moist, stale breath, he stirred, squinted open his eyes, and waked smiling.

"Why did you marry me?" I asked.

"So I could wake up to you every day." He stretched and reached for me. I scooted away, then leapt out of bed and flung on my clothes.

That afternoon, Marc set up his camera on a tripod, then frolicked naked in the Ninnescah River. Shallow water ballooned my baggy T-shirt and shorts as I sat reading. Eight pages from the end of a romance novel I'd found at a downtown Harper drugstore, I watched Marc leap into the air and press the camera's remote control. In pictures that have since been lost, Marc is naked and free and always in motion, with me in the background, clothed, cringing, and shielding my face from his splashes.

I am married, I thought, watching a shape dart through the water, a small fish, dark and fleeting. I am a married woman.

The day before I'd been a college senior who lived with my parents. Now I was a married woman. My transition from childhood to adulthood had come about with the jarring suddenness of that of my old Growing Up Skipper doll, who arrived in her box flat-chested, but when you twisted her arm, breasts appeared.

Marc crawled toward me like a stalking animal preparing to pounce. "Stop!" I shrieked, laughing, as he leapt through the air and covered me with puppy dog kisses. My dread was back. I pushed him away. "Don't," I said.

"This is our honeymoon," he protested.

I stared down into the clear water and lied. "I forgot my pills."

Marc pulled back. I couldn't stand to look at the hurt on his face.

"We don't want to risk getting pregnant," I said. We'd talked about children; Marc didn't want to father any. There was a one in ten chance of passing on ankylosing spondylitis. Someday, we'd agreed, we would adopt or have a test tube baby or something—someday far in the future.

"I'll get something at the drugstore," Marc said.

More tiny fish streamed by.

"If you want me to, I mean," Marc said.

"Well, we're *married*," was all I could think of to answer, giddy at even a brief reprieve.

That seemed to reassure him. He crouched low and crept toward me again.

"When do you think we'll have kids?" I asked.

Abruptly subdued, Marc lowered himself to sit beside me in the water. "I don't know," he said. "I thought we already talked about this. I don't know if I really want any."

"I mean, adopt them or something."

"Maybe in ten or fifteen years." He shrugged. "I'm not mature enough to be a father. I don't know if I ever will be."

"Never?" I said. We'd talked about this subject months ago. He'd do whatever I wanted, he'd said, desperate for me to marry him. He pulled out my chair at the dinner table, every week he brought me flowers wrapped in green tissue paper, and we sat up in the window of his apartment while church bells tolled nearby and he pleaded with me and made promises. We'd have babies someday, and he'd come with us to church. Now, married one day, a life I didn't want stretched before me, a childless one of deflecting my husband's advances.

Nearly thirty years later, I remember this honeymoon, this marriage, as if they were fiction, things I made up.

Now, the mother of a teenager, no longer a churchgoer, I wish I had the photos to show my daughter. In one, I remember, I huddled around my book, all pale long limbs, while a spray of droplets flew up behind Marc, who had just splashed away. In another picture, Marc cartwheeled through the water, caught upside down, arms flung out, eyes and mouth wide, exaggerated astonishment, showing off for an invisible audience.

I wish I could somehow cross the years and say to the girl in the water, the girl who no longer exists even in photographs, You will be okay. You will grow older and braver and travel the world and raise a daughter, and Marc will raise a daughter of his own, both girls named Sophie: wisdom. I wish I could time travel to the past to rescue that girl who thought she was rescuing me, my middle-aged self, from spinsterhood, from hell. You will be okay, I want to say, but maybe she really did save me, in ways I can't fully fathom. My Sophie looks at pictures of my younger self. My Sophie rolls her eyes. She is scornful. She cannot conceive of willfully throwing away her own life. Knowing this, I feel both diminished in her eyes and secretly triumphant that I have taught her to value her own life as she does.

Looking at wedding pictures, I can't begin to imagine or remember what that girl was thinking, in those pictures or later, staring past the book at the river's wind-rippled current that polished small stones, tangled plants in its sway, and blurred infinite dark fish, so fast they always seemed to be fleeing. The camera shutter whirred and Marc's feet pushed against the current. Overhead an airplane left a vapor trail like a pipe cleaner, firm spine, fuzzy edges.

What I do remember is tamping down panic as I lowered my book into the water, pages turning heavy and inseparable. It briefly reduced the enormity of what I'd done to consider this problem before me, whether I would be able to peel apart the pages and read the ending, whether I even cared.

Marc clicked the remote. I recall a photo showing him standing on his hands in the shallows. Somewhere, beyond the frame, I was panicking, feeling surreal, wondering how I got to this place. In the photo, you could see, just barely, my book, partially submerged, the title unreadable, bobbing along in the water, floating on past.

Can This Marriage Be Saved? A Quiz

8. Why have you fought to keep your marriage together all these years?

a. When you walked down the aisle on your father's arm, all
the guests were tittering. Your husband-to-be stood before them in a tuxedo and high-top sneakers, dyed black.
You told yourself that you loved his humor, even if at that
moment he was too busy scanning the audience, enjoying
his joke, to watch you. You felt unreal anyway, as if you
were only masquerading as a bride. Later you and your
husband cut the cake and you threw the bouquet, which
bounced off the low ceiling, uncaught. And then the skies
opened and everyone clapped and cheered, because rain
on the day of a wedding was good luck. Secretly you felt
beyond the influence of luck, unreal, like a character in
someone else's story, speeding into an unknown dark
future. You stared at your bright little star of a diamond
and remembered from astronomy class why it was impossible to travel faster than the speed of light: something
about gaining mass the faster you went, slowing yourself
down. But if you didn't rush ahead accumulating the
weight of all of your regrets, who knew where you would
find yourself?

b. Even when the two of you argued because he came home
too late, smelling of beer and smoke, you were married.

c. He missed your family birthday dinner, leaving you to blow out candles and make excuses for him, but you still took marriage seriously.

d. When his mother frowned at your piles of books, your stacks and tumbles of books, and you felt like a slovenly, promiscuous, gluttonous reader wallowing there, and you understood there was a standard you could never live up to, you reminded yourself that you weren't married to *her*. You told yourself that again when she rearranged your haphazard place settings, replaced folded paper towels with white cloth napkins, and shooed you away from overzealously whipping the mashed potatoes. She wore a supernaturally unwrinkled linen jacket and tapped polished nails against the counter. You looked at your own bitten nails and thought how insignificant her judgment was compared to the real problem: You had no desire for her son. But you were married, and you were religious, and you didn't want to feel like a failure, and none of this was easily undone.

e. When his disease flared, it bowed him like an old man, and you understood how it felt to have your body betray you, your own body that attracted unwanted attention when you were young, your body that will not cooperate with you now in your mind's deception that everything is okay in your marriage. On your honeymoon, the way your body seized up with tension during sex was understandable. But it never stopped hurting, as if your body had a will of its own, as if it was outright refusing to give in. Bewildered by your intense, inexplicable pain, your husband withdrew. He said that his arthritis was flaring up anyway. And so there you were, both of you, with bodies that fended off normality, and you might as well be abnormal together, you thought.

f. You convinced yourself that you were responsible for the stress that aggravated his disease. To look behind him, your husband twisted his whole torso. To reach a low shelf, he climbed on a stool. He waved his hand out the window of his Toyota truck, vowing to get more exercise to keep his muscles from freezing. He didn't like being fussed over, but you stood by, trying to help, trying to repair the damage you had caused.

g. When you longed for your first love, and other, more flexible men, you felt even guiltier.

h. But your husband still made you laugh. He was goofy, a practical joker, the kind who left messages for coworkers on April Fool's Day: "Call Mrs. Lyon," he'd write, or "Call Mr. Bayer," with the number for the zoo. When his sister asked him to arrange the tables before her wedding reception, he and his brother spelled out the word "sex" and she was too preoccupied to notice, not clued in until her wedding guests welcomed her to the reception with uproarious laughter. When your husband conducted an editorial-page phone survey about aerosol sprays, he polled only people from a town called Ozone. For opinions about rape legislation, he interviewed residents of Cherry Hill and Pencil Bluff. His flippancy about this survey made you a little uneasy, and you realized that the mildly amusing entertainment he offered was a thin basis for a marriage. But it was what you had, so you laughed.

i. When he talked about divorce, you were afraid. You didn't know what would become of you.

BREATHING ON YOUR OWN
Tips for Breaking That Nasal Spray Addiction

MAYBE IT STARTS with a cold, allergies, hay fever—at any rate, you're stuffy and congested, and maybe all night you sniffle and snort and toss and turn and bounce off the bed to pace, hoping that gravity will clear your sinuses. Let's say that you're twenty years old, newly married, though probably it's just a coincidence that your inability to breathe kicked in right after the wedding.

Maybe your new husband, the son of a pharmacist, compares your nighttime breathing patterns to the rumble of a Mack truck (affectionately, of course). And maybe he offers you a topical nasal decongestant and says, "Try this." Maybe you're dubious, but he assures you that he has it on his dad's good authority that you should ignore the warnings on the container, the ones that caution you not to use it for more than three days.

So now, you're twenty years old and you're hooked. Say that not too long ago you were a girl who went to church every Sunday and never swore, a girl whose biggest rebellion was memorizing the *Jesus Christ Superstar* soundtrack after your youth minister warned you away from it. And now the beginning of your marriage has handed you disillusionment after disillusionment. Your husband mocks religion and drinks beer at lunch and never has time for a real conversation.

And now you're an addict. You don't even drink and you've never smoked. You've always been an advocate of natural highs, the kind you get from stroking a purring cat or watching snow fall or listening to music or reading a great poem, but now here you are, dependent on a little plastic bottle, unable to breathe without it. You always thought that addiction required a high, but now you know that sometimes all it takes is the blessed absence of pain or struggle. And it's such a relief to sleep deeply through the night. It's such a relief not to flip from side to side or start awake, face to face with your regrets.

With proper rest, you feel less despair about this whole mess you've gotten yourself into, this short-term cure, this escape that might be a bigger trap after all—the marriage, not the nasal spray. Maybe you entered this marriage with deliberate recklessness, sad and lost and scared of your bleak, blank future when the boy you'd grown up with and loved for six years broke up with you abruptly and eventually moved away, disappeared. Maybe you'd foolishly believed that marriage would provide a refuge from your anxiety, that somehow it would allow you to breathe again. But no. Here you are, and every time you inhale a squirt of medicine and feel a rush of fresh air through your open passages, you know that you're just delaying the inevitable, that time is closing in on you. At first you just need it once a day, but soon it's twice, three times. The spray temporarily shrinks your swelled blood vessels, but then causes them to swell up twice as big the next time. You push down panic but still it's like you're inhaling and exhaling to the same refrain: What will you do? What will you do? What are you going to do?

What follow are some guidelines for breaking that addiction gradually but effectively.

1. Identify your danger zones.

So you're twenty years old and newly married, and you can't drive your husband's stick shift, or work his complicated stereo, or light the gas range, or squeeze anything but one ice cube tray into the frost-packed freezer. And that panic, that now familiar panic, rises up again so that your thoughts are all clogged and congested and you can't breathe and you think, What am I doing here? How did I end up here? How is this my life?

A week later, you're arguing with your husband about him smoking hash in the basement. You argue about him going straight from work to hang out with his friends at Kirby's bar till midnight. You argue because the evenings he does come home, he disappears again with his camera, reappearing only to grab some equipment, a tripod to shoot a guy playing Hacky Sack on a median strip at rush hour, a lens to photograph a hooker at a downtown hotel. After you fight, he usually apologizes, promises to call, to come home earlier. He doesn't. After the really big fights, he brings you flowers.

And you keep turning to nasal spray, as if it will free you from your constrictions. If only you can breathe, you think, everything will be all right.

2. Employ alternative coping skills.

Try calming breathing exercises to release your tension, unless, of course, those exercises call attention to your congestion. Get fresh air. Exercise. Seek solace in music. Sing the *Jesus Christ Superstar* soundtrack at the top of your lungs, even if your former youth director complained that in it Jesus is erratic and egotistical and inappropriately involved with Mary Magdalene, even if the apostles are only concerned with their own fame, even if Jesus says that, for all they care, the wine and bread might as well be his blood and body, calling into question that whole transubstantiation thing.

Listen to records, your husband's Pink Floyd and Janis Ian and David Bowie and Bonnie Raitt and Bob Dylan, since your husband convinced you to sell most of your own childhood favorites in his mother's garage sale. He and Kirk argued persuasively if somewhat drunkenly that your Barry Manilows and ABBAs so violated the limits of good taste, their very presence threatened to stigmatize you both, forcing you to become outcasts. Was keeping them really fair to your husband and his reputation?

You also agreed to jettison the Carpenters, which you have clung to fiercely ever since your youth director burned his. He'd realized that they were distractions from his faith and built a big bonfire to destroy all temptation. You puzzle over how these songs could corrupt anyone:

because they suggest that angels have nothing better to do than create a dreamboat guy for all the girls to swoon over? Because it sounds like Karen Carpenter is attempting to usurp the place of God when she sings about being on top of the world, looking down on creation, giddy at being in love? You've hung onto your Simon and Garfunkel, and you listen to those records over and over, crinoline of smoky burgundy, a bow tie that's really a camera, you are a rock, you are an island. Sometimes the speakers fall over and voices go on singing, muffled, music trapped there in the carpet.

You find a children's record in your husband's collection and play "I'm a Lonely Little Petunia in an Onion Patch" repeatedly until he hides it. You play his Janis Ian album, morose songs accompanied by dramatic violins, learning the truth at seventeen that love was meant for beauty queens. "Depressed again?" your husband says whenever he sees the Janis Ian album cover out. You like it that he gets you in this one way, that he can so accurately gauge your moods through the music you're listening to.

Your husband's favorite albums tend toward the loud and throbbing. They pound like someone hacking a hole through the wall. Despite that, despite the fact that he's gotten you addicted to nasal spray, he will also get you hooked, over the years, on Joni Mitchell, the Eurythmics, Suzanne Vega, Fleetwood Mac, 10,000 Maniacs, Nanci Griffith.

3. Face your feelings instead of avoiding them.

When, at night, you sit up waiting for the phone to ring or your husband's truck to roar into the driveway, acknowledge your sadness. Remember that you've always felt a sadness, especially at dusk, that has nothing to do with your marriage or your struggle to breathe or the absence of your husband. You've weathered this sadness a million times. Recall, in that gaping chasm between late afternoon and darkness, as you head into another evening alone, how your mom used to watch Lawrence Welk on Saturday nights. You used to hear it in the background with a restless sense that somewhere beyond these songs, beyond the dusk closing in, there was music with serrated edges that could slice right through you.

Your mom preferred this sweet, sanitized stuff, and you'll be surprised many years later, after both of your parents' deaths, to find hundreds of sexy cards they exchanged on birthdays and Valentine's Days. You will feel weirdly betrayed by these cards, with double entendres and racy jokes, so opposite the pure, chaste pecks on the lips they gave each other, their only visible displays of affection. You will feel misled, as if it's finally occurring to you that you shouldn't have married someone for whom you feel so little attraction. Maybe if you'd known about the cards, you would be with someone who wildly attracted you, less taken in by your mom's careful appearance of sexlessness, by this Lawrence Welk vision of courtship and marriage. Women's skirts swirled before life-size plastic trees as they whirled and sang, "Don't sit under the apple tree with anyone else but me." Another woman perched on a couch arm while a man gazed benevolently down on her and they harmonized on "It's Nice to Have a Man Around the House." That same couple, or maybe another equally fresh-faced one, joined together in a duet of "Let's Call the Whole Thing Off." Because this selection was in honor of National Library Week, they turned the pages of large dictionaries on stands while they sang, "You say to-may-to, I say to-mah-to."

Remember that dusk has made you anxious since childhood, has always been the time that you've fretted about what will become of you. Long ago, stranded in the abyss between twilight and daylight, between childhood and adulthood, you were relieved when darkness finally fell and instrumental renditions of songs like "Hey Jude" flushed out couples in tuxes and ballgowns. They slow danced while the lights above them spelled out "Geritol." Soon the whole cast assembled for a chorus of "Till We Meet Again," and the day was safely over.

4. Don't be discouraged by setbacks.

Maybe after the first month, you wean yourself from nasal spray. Then two months later, you give in again to your longing to breathe. You promise yourself that you'll break the habit as soon as things settle down, and it seems that they might. After all, when he forgets your birthday altogether, your remorseful husband promises to turn over a new leaf and stay home more. He brings you carnations. He hauls in brown bags of food. He unloads them and clatters pots and pans. He pops into the living room to turn the Allman Brothers on loud. You sort laundry, waiting for pauses in the music, listening for the cheerful noises of the house that have been humming all along beneath the pounding bass. A spoon scraping against a bowl, the sound of the furnace kicking on. You breathe in the smells of cheese and basil and tomatoes.

By dinnertime, your husband has spread out a white linen tablecloth and wedding-present placemats. He arranges bowls of green salad, glasses of red wine. He spoons up stuffed manicotti and browned sauce. He serves

French bread in a basket, sliced and buttered and toasted with fresh garlic.

You tell him that it's the best dinner anyone has ever made for you, and it's true. But there's a bitter, medicinal undercurrent to every bite. Resolve again to stop using nasal spray. Try not to dread your husband's garlic kisses.

5. Solicit support from family and friends, but lower your expectations, accepting gratefully whatever they are able to give.

Newly twenty-one, you could be susceptible to believing that the seemingly vast cultural rift between you and your husband's family is a sign of your inferiority. Your mother-in-law asks you to pick up some Pall Mall cigarettes on the way to her house for dinner, and, misunderstanding, you bring her Palmolive dish soap. You have no clue that when your husband's dad died a couple of years ago, she found cocaine among his socks. What you see is the perfect surface of her life, with her high thread count sheets and salon shampoos. What you see are her pursed lips as she fixes the table where you have tossed silverware beside each plate and gathered paper towels to serve as napkins. Sighing, she separates the knives and spoons from the forks and places them equidistant from the edges of the plates and placemats. Counting out cloth napkins, she rolls her eyes at your husband.

But so what if neither she nor your husband tolerates wood veneer, cakes made from mixes, mashed potatoes from flakes, synthetic bags, or polyester blends. So what if she would never use garlic powder instead of fresh cloves or make pizza crust from canned biscuits. Never mind that she decorates her bathroom with arrangements of molded soap, intricate flowers and seashells that your husband warns you not to use. Somehow the cracks and crevices of their elaborate patterns remain sharp, neither worn down by use nor outlined by dust. Big deal if there's never a ring in your mother-in-law's bathtub, never a layer of dust on top of her oak china hutch, never a smudge on the front hallway's mirrored tiles that deliver back to you endless repetitions of yourself.

Maybe you're reluctant to confess your misery to your own mother and you consider leaning on your coworkers. But at the campus yearbook, where you're the office manager and a staff writer, you're no longer the boss's girlfriend, someone to impress and woo. Now you're the nagging harpy trying to stand in the way of your husband's fun. "Buddy, you're losing weight," you hear Kirk, now serving as his coeditor, say. "Isn't she feeding you enough?"

"He's gained ten pounds," you growl, and all the guys scatter like crows in response to a hurled rock. But he *has* gained weight. You know this because he accused you of shrinking his jeans, and his mother said to you reprovingly, "You should never dry jeans," and then, weeks later, he sheepishly confessed that he'd gone to buy replacements and discovered that he no longer fit into the same size.

A layout guy stops in at the office with his three-year-old daughter. "This is Marc's wife," he introduces you.

"And a person in her own right," you chirp.

Later, Kirk reprimands you for your hostile knee-jerk reaction. "Do you have a problem with being Marc's wife?" he asks.

Turn to your friends for support. They mean well, even if they are, like you, young and mystified by the idea of marriage, even if they've stopped inviting you places because they assume you are busy doing whatever married people do. "Wedded bliss!" they shriek when you see them on campus. "Look at her glow!" they crow. "You're gaining weight," they say, nudging each other, eyebrows raised knowingly about the cause of your supposed fat, happy state. You've actually lost ten pounds and developed constant stomachaches, but you smile weakly. You don't let on that you're finding marriage to be a pretty odd concept, that it feels like you're impersonating someone who has been admitted into an exalted secret society full of romance and mystery. You feel inadequate, embarrassed, sure that you're the only bride on earth whose marriage is a sham, the only one who has no idea whatsoever how to be a wife.

So maybe you don't quite know how to talk about this. Resist the temptation to instead lean on a drug that clears your sinuses and allows you to sleep at night, to forget about all of this for a few unconscious hours.

6. Recognize the patterns that keep defeating you and quit making excuses.

Every few months, as if he's scheduled it, your husband grows silent and restless. "We shouldn't have gotten married," he says. "I just thought it would be like having a roommate you have sex with. I don't want to be married anymore." You make promises, resolving not to limit his freedom. And when he accepts a job as a newspaper photographer in Pratt, Kansas, an hour away, you support him. You stay in Wichita for a semester to finish school, then defer graduate school and join him.

Soon after, he gets restless, says it again: "I don't want to be married." You leave for two days, staying with a friend. When you finally call your husband, he pleads with you to come back. You're so congested from crying that you turn to nasal spray again. It takes you a month to get off of it. Notice how your marriage, your addiction, cycle together: you're congested, he feels all hemmed in, he explodes, you go back on nasal spray. He apologizes and makes promises, you go cold turkey and, finally freed of the medicine, you breathe without help. Your husband is kind and solicitous, and you think that your marriage might make it, and then the whole cycle repeats itself.

You never ask exactly what it would mean for your marriage to make it or whether you really want to stay together forever. All you know is that the idea of navigating life on your own is terrifying.

7. Forget about yourself and do things for others.

If, say, you don't feel especially attracted to your husband, instead of retreating and refusing to communicate, try cultivating intimacy. Develop a repertoire of back massages, for instance. Pioneer the Singing Back Rub, performed to selections from *Mary Poppins* and excerpts from "Bohemian Rhapsody." Devise a Reciting Back Rub in which you recall stray lines from poems memorized in school: "Annabel Lee," "The Night before Christmas," and the "O that this too too solid flesh would melt, thaw, and resolve itself into a dew" speech from *Hamlet*. Create the Olympic Commentator Back Rub, in which you replay and analyze your own daring moves: "Well, Peggy, that first run down the spine was pretty adventurous for a newcomer. Yes, Dick, and did you see how seamlessly she moved into a three-fingered jab followed by a full-knuckle punch?"

Be pleased by the way your husband smiles drowsily, dozing off.

8. Take joy in your talents and abilities. Develop new hobbies and interests. Take a class. Gain confidence in your own worth and rights.

First, take inventory of what you do well. Say, playing "Baby Elephant Walk" fast on the piano. Pointing your toes, which you can do like a ballerina because your feet are double-jointed.

Learn to trust your own vision and interpretations. Say your husband claims that every tall building was modeled after the male anatomy; that women's earrings are a manifestation of penis envy, imitating the only thing in nature that dangles; that every song in existence is directly related to male body parts. Maybe, while listening to Jackson Browne, for instance, he says, "You know who Rosie is, don't you?"

"She wears his ring—his wife?" you venture.

"Rosie is his dick," your husband says authoritatively. "Get it? 'I've got to hand it to me'?" He snickers. Many years later, a boyfriend will argue that Rosie is his hand. "Ick," you will say both times, wondering why anyone would listen to this song more than once, after the joke wears off.

Maybe you don't feel worthwhile, or like you have rights, since you don't bring in much money from your own part-time jobs. Because of this, you may hesitate over purchases—a loaf of bread, a Sunday newspaper. Maybe you resent the easy way your husband drops money on records, but you're grateful too. You play Bruce Springsteen's *Born in the USA* and Cyndi Lauper's *She's So Unusual* over and over. You wish to be one of those carefree girls with their straightforward yearnings in "Girls Just Want to Have Fun." You're drawn to the slow wistfulness and tenderness and lusty longing of "All Through the Night." In "I'm on Fire," Bruce Springsteen, hoarse and raw and close to the bone, desperate with desire, wakes up your nerve endings.

Your husband says that Lauper's cover of Prince's "When You Were Mine," is about group oral sex. "What did you think she meant by those references to trains and eating?" he asks.

You feel hopelessly naïve. You'd been willing to believe that it was about Amtrak and dining cars.

"You know what *Blueboy* magazines are, don't you?" he says when "She Bop" plays. "You know why she jokes that she might go blind?"

You've been picturing the Gainsborough painting *The Blue Boy*, which hung in your parents' living room above the couch. You long for the innocence of that world.

And then your husband goes too far, claiming that "All Through the Night" is about prostitution. "Once we start, the meter clicks?" he says, wiggling his eyebrows.

This time, you argue. You insist that prostitutes do not charge for their services like cab drivers. You argue that it's a romantic song about a night that feels outside of time and ordinary concerns. You remember feeling this way about your first boyfriend, wanting evenings with him to last forever. You don't mention this. Instead you maintain that the meter is a metaphor for the way that the reality of passing time and the knowledge of the inevitable end of pleasure and happiness haunts every moment. You tell your husband that he is dead wrong.

9. Seek professional help.

"Get a real addiction," your friends say, laughing, but consult a doctor anyway. He will scold you; it may be true, he says, that compared with, say, alcohol or cocaine or heroin, nasal spray is cheap and readily available, doesn't threaten your reputation or your credit rating, alter your judgment, impair your logic, or lead you into dangerous parts of town.

You are nevertheless in the grip of a real addiction, he tells you. He orders you to go cold turkey. He advises salt water spray, a humidifier. He prescribes steroids. He says words that will forever after strike you as profound: "Both nostrils will never naturally close at the same time. Remember that one nostril is always open. Breathe through that one."

You are reminded of that old saying, about how when God closes one door, He opens another. When it comes to your nose, you infinitely prefer for all the doors to be open. But you resolve to give up the nasal spray once and for all.

10. Take control of your own life. Go cold turkey forever.

Someday you'll be brave enough for this. To leave behind the nasal spray, the marriage. To challenge your husband when he tells you that Suzanne Vega's "Gypsy," a song about a fleeting love with a free spirit, is about a penis. "A long and slender body and a bump upon the head?" he will say.

Roll your eyes. Say, "It is not about a penis."

"Then how do you explain that line?" your husband will ask.

"I don't know," you answer. "Unless the guy has a long and slender body and has actually bumped his head."

Listen to this song over and over, and the Eurythmics' "The Miracle of Love," and know that you need something more than what you have.

Gather your courage. The courage to keep saying to your husband, "It is not," when he tells you that everything is about the male anatomy. The courage to say, when your husband tells you he doesn't want to be married anymore, "Neither do I." The courage to fend off dread and anxiety, your forehead and palms turning clammy as you wonder how you will ever do anything on your own. The courage to toss every nasal spray bottle into a dumpster, pitching them hard and fast between bulging plastic bags and rotten fruit swarming with flies, to hear them rattle down into places where you'll never be tempted to follow them. Eventually, someday, maybe far in the future, you'll find the courage for all of this. The courage to lie on your couch then, and breathe.

It will take you a long, long time to get there. Years. You will face many obstacles first. Right now, you have a ways to go.

But know that someday, you'll manage it: your doubts will shrink, will float away. You'll breathe.

You'll focus on your open nostril rather than your closed one. You'll feel very Zen.

You'll breathe with what you have.

WHAT SURVIVES

May 1984

THE DAY AFTER Marc announces, for the third time, that he doesn't want to be married, he calls me from the doctor's office.

"They think I have cancer," he says.

I am twenty-one. We've been married for less than a year. I'm still using nasal spray, on for a month, off for six or seven months, on again for weeks at a time. It's a cycle. Everything is a cycle.

Absently, I pet the cat, whose sides bulge with unborn kittens. She came to us scrawny, almost weightless, mewing pitifully, and before we'd saved up enough money to get her fixed, she was pregnant.

If we can't afford to get a cat fixed, how will we afford cancer, I wonder, twisting the spiraling phone cord around my finger, encasing it. And yet I feel, shamefully, a sense of resignation and relief. Cancer will bind us together. Now I can't leave Marc, and he can't leave me.

I've always been aware, of course, of Marc's ankylosing spondylitis, the disease he first explained to me as like arthritis in his spine. He rarely complains about it, so it has taken me months of living with him to understand what a central fact of his life it is, though it ebbs and flows, going through cycles.

Ankylosing spondylitis is an incurable autoimmune disease that inflames the joints of the spine, and in addition to back pain, sufferers often experience pain in the pelvis, shoulders, or hips and are more prone to uveitis or iritis, an inflammation of the eyes. Some people have long periods of remission and, ultimately, minimal disability, while others experience increasingly reduced flexibility of the spine and thus reduced mobility. There is no way of knowing what effect the disease will have on Marc over the long term, and I'm not sure whether he's had more flare-ups since our marriage or rather that because we live together, it's harder for him to conceal them from me. What I do know is that the pain pills make him mercurial, and he's complained a lot more lately about being stiff and sore, drawing hot baths twice a day, moving slowly. Although he is only twenty-eight, when the disease flares, he walks bowed like an old man. Lately, his eye has swollen as another bout of iritis sets in. "I don't know what part of this disease is worse," he says. Daily he says, "I hate my body."

His disease is beginning to feel like a metaphor for our marriage, which has felt infected from the start, caught up in its own cycle. Periodically he starts to pull away, turns distant. I worry, we argue, he announces he doesn't want to be married, I panic, he brings me flowers and apologizes. Maybe getting married was his idea, maybe I resisted it for a long time, but now that we are, I'm determined to make it work, convinced that I'm to blame for any difficulties.

I offer him back rubs, suggest hot baths, fetch his pain pills, encourage him to exercise, try to understand when he snaps at me, but mostly I feel helpless to do anything for him. He chafes at too much attention, but it seems wrong to not acknowledge when he's in pain. And I worry constantly that my expectations are unreasonable, my belief that a little more romance and attention might alleviate some of my pain during sex, my insistence that he call me if he's not going to be home for dinner or that he not disappear for whole evenings. I worry that my demands, the things I always thought were givens in a marriage, are stressing him out and making his disease worse.

In the months since the honeymoon, I've been making excuses, looking for reprieves from sex, which ranges from excruciatingly painful to severely uncomfortable. Many years later, I will be finally diagnosed with endometriosis, which, like Marc's disease, can be exacerbated by stress, but for the duration of my marriage, I will remain puzzled by my body's resistance and by sex's failure to live up to its reputation. And I will be convinced that there's something seriously wrong with me, that I can never lead a normal life, will feel a constant sense of dread about my future.

August 1983–April 1984

Soon after the wedding, I suggested that maybe we needed to see a counselor about the sex thing. We were driving in a rainstorm. Drops fell fast, shattering across the road in front of us like beads spilling from a broken necklace.

"No one else has ever complained." Marc flicked on the windshield wipers, then clicked them off again. He hated the sound of rubber scraping against a dry window. His habit of constantly turning the switch on and off made him seem even moodier than usual.

"How many people have you slept with?" I asked.

"Oh, I don't know, fifteen," he said.

"Wow. Fifteen?"

He smiled like I'd just paid him a compliment.

This number of successful encounters struck me as confirmation that the problems we were having were indeed my fault. When I mentioned them to my childhood family practitioner, he looked embarrassed. "You just need to relax," he said. My gynecologist thought I might have a yeast infection and prescribed suppositories. A general practitioner recommended by my mom gave me a book on God's view of a wife's role. None of these solutions alleviated the wretched pain of sex.

Old novels I'd devoured since childhood had been populated by stern characters who frowned at vanity and arrogance and took as their mottos sayings like *Practice makes perfect* or *If at first you don't succeed, try, try again.* These heroines extolled the importance of inner beauty, knowing that the truly virtuous were attracted to the kind, loyal hearts of others, not repelled by superficial things like hairy toes or coffee breath.

I resolved to make my marriage work, throwing myself into it as if it were a math problem, as if I could figure out the right answers, erase my mistakes, and add it all up to a sum beyond searing pain. But then Marc started rebuffing my advances. "I'm kind of sore," he said. "Stress makes my arthritis worse."

Relief reverted to guilt: I was causing his flare-up.

"So tell me about the fifteen," I said. I plumped up my pillow and turned to face him.

"The fifteen what?" He yawned.

"The women. The ones you slept with. What were their names?"

He groaned, but he was smiling. "I don't remember," he said.

"You don't remember their names?"

"Well, not all of them."

"Tell me the ones you remember."

"You're not supposed to ask questions like this," he said. "Can you rub my back?"

I sat up, tentatively kneading his shoulders. He lifted and dropped them appreciatively. Carefully, I rubbed along his spine.

"Harder," he said.

I imagined pounding bread dough, punching bed pillows into place, scrubbing the side of our stained bathtub with all my might, patting potting soil around flowers, being good at domestic things.

"How did you meet them?" I asked.

"Meet who?"

"The fifteen."

"It's not like I met them all at the same time."

"Well, how did you meet each one?"

"How am I supposed to remember all this?"

"How could you not remember?"

He foggily recounted seductions at music festivals and liaisons on the job. Of his lineup of lovers, I might be the least experienced, but at least we knew each other pretty well, comparatively, I thought.

I absently goaded him as he called up an array of food-related words for female body parts: *taco, clam, muff burger, butterbean.*

"Did they give good back rubs?" I asked as his voice trailed off toward sleep.

"Who?" he asked.

"The fifteen."

"No," he said. "You're the best." He lifted and lowered his shoulders in an exaggerated sigh of contentment. "I like being in love."

This didn't last long. Within a few weeks after the wedding, restlessness had set in. He complained: he hadn't realized that marriage meant being accountable to another person. He hated the way I did things, like that I never folded underwear, just wadded it into a drawer. His mother used to not only fold his shorts, she had ironed them first.

I tiptoed around him, wondering if I was going to have to start ironing underwear to save my marriage. I felt spacey, weirdly hormonal, retreating into daydreams about Cole. I wondered if his old house was still the barn red color he'd painted it the spring we were juniors, when I'd always been picking red brown flecks from his dark hair. I dug out old photo albums and yearbooks; we had once shot a whole roll of film of each other, varying the settings. In the pictures, Cole rummaged through lettuce in my dad's garden, pretended to turn cartwheels on the sidewalk in front of our garage, tried on my older brother's helmet and posed in front of his motorcycle. His face looked so young and I couldn't recall the sound of his voice. I stared at the picture, trying to remember what it had felt like to kiss him and be swept away by desire.

Early in our marriage, when Marc hung out at bars after work and came home later and later and we argued and he announced that he didn't want to be married, I didn't stop to think about what I wanted. Did *I* want to be married to him? It wasn't a question I could bring myself to consider. I was married, and what I wanted didn't matter. I'd been raised to take commitment seriously, and deep down, I couldn't imagine life on my own, where I'd live, how I'd support myself, how I'd navigate the awkwardness of dating.

Marc had felt guilty, brought me flowers, turned kind, solicitous. We'd laughed a lot for a few weeks, until the distance opened up between us again.

I joined a Bible study, trying to prove to myself that I hadn't given up on my beliefs even though Marc and I didn't go to church. I signed up for a group in time to catch the tail end of the Life and Letters of Paul and was glad to have missed the discussion of women remaining silent in church and obeying their husbands. But now I was stumbling into a new minefield with the study of Matthew and the Bible's teachings on marriage, divorce, and the single life. I focused on appearing normal, like there weren't deep fault lines in my marriage already, after only a few months.

It was that winter that Marc got the job offer in Pratt, Kansas, a small town loomed over by two water towers labeled "hot" and "cold," the kind of prank Marc would play. Jobs for newspaper photographers were scarce, and for Marc, this felt like a coup, a first step to the career he'd always dreamed of, and so I agreed to postpone graduate school in order to move there with him. We lived apart for two months while I finished school in Wichita, lonely living in our apartment by myself, nervous alone there at night. Then I joined him in Pratt.

At first, we were happy to be reunited, though he was a little alarmed when I brought the cat home. "You don't want to keep it, do you?" he asked. The next day he came home with a ten-pound bag of Happy Cat and a litter box.

After that, he kept dancing Kitty around the living room, singing, "What makes you so bad? You weren't brought up that way."

"It's like we're a whole family now," he said. "Mom, Dad, and the Kid."

Soon after, our family expanded further when he brought home his family's dog, a malamute his mother no longer wanted to take care of.

May 1984

The day Marc calls me from Wichita to tell me he might have cancer, we've been on a downhill trend. How, in so little time, has he moved from dancing the kitty around the room to withdrawing from me, acting like I'm a nuisance, flinching when I speak to him? He often retreats to the basement to work on his clip file, slicing photographs out of newspapers with an X-Acto blade, discarded strips snowing around him. He hums along with the music that pounds through the ceiling, more hammering than tune.

This is it, I've been thinking with dread, the climax of our repeating cycle: he doesn't want to be married anymore.

And then he said, "I'm going to Wichita tonight. I have my checkup in the morning. I keep thinking I ought to wait till the health insurance kicks in, but Mother insists." He didn't suggest that I come along.

I spent the afternoon and evening forgetting to eat, giving up any hope of concentration. And then comes the call. The one in which he tells me he might have cancer.

"Where are you?" I ask.

"At the hospital," he says. "The doctor insisted I go to a urologist, and the urologist wouldn't let me leave till I made an appointment to come here for tests."

"Why?" I shift gears abruptly from wronged to concerned wife.

"He found a spot on my kidney. He won't say the word cancer, but I can tell he's thinking it. He wants me to check into the hospital right away. He wants to put me out and do exploratory surgery. But we can't afford it. We don't have insurance."

"How much will it cost? When will we have insurance?" I'm ashamed at how much better I feel, now that we're united in purpose together. I clutch the phone as he explains something about a six-week waiting period for new employees and something else about pre-existing conditions. He breaks off. "I don't want to have cancer," he says.

"We'll figure it out," I say. Normally, he chafes at any attempts I make to be solicitous, as if acknowledgement of his disease is akin to suggesting that he's defective. He also tends to subvert emotional intimacy with jokes. But right now he needs me in a way he never has before, and I know how to be supportive. As scary as the possibility of cancer is, I feel a weird relief because at least, for once, I understand my role, how to be a wife. I imagine, in fifty years, telling our children and grandchildren that this was the turning point in our marriage, the moment that we became true partners.

Marc arrives home from his doctor visits contrite, the tension and anger of the last few days faded. We talk about our options. The hospital gave him an estimate, thousands of dollars we don't have. His mother offered to pay, but he's too proud to take her up on it. If we can bide our time for a few weeks, he insists, the tests will be covered.

I don't think we should wait, but I don't see what choice we have.

In the Sunday paper, I stall on an article about recovery rates for different types of cancer. Cancer of the kidney, caught early, has a pretty high survival rate. I imagine my future as a devoted wife, driving Marc back and forth to Wichita for treatments, feeding him and bringing him medications and books and magazines. I can do all of this.

Marc comes in from outside, hair damp with sweat. He's wearing a sleeveless T-shirt, showing all the muscles in his arms. He always insists he isn't very strong, but right now, though he carries his back carefully, though we both are consumed by worry, he looks tan and fit.

"I've decided to plant a garden," he announces. "What do you think about corn? And radishes grow pretty fast, and I want cucumbers for pickles."

I'm happy that he has thrown himself into a distraction. That afternoon, I watch him guide a rototiller, churning up earth in the backyard. The tiny garden plot seems silly, an ineffectual spot of brown among weeds and sky, but if it's his way of not thinking about cancer, I will pretend for his sake that it's a lush paradise.

Anxiety turns him more affectionate, strangling my hand with his as we take long walks down brick streets. "I don't want to have cancer," he keeps saying, the mantra that has replaced, "I don't want to be married."

He tells me that he's going to exercise more regularly to keep from stiffening up so much. For a couple of nights, he has gone to run up and down the stadium stairs a block from our house, but now a front is coming in and he's even more sore than usual.

I trace the rash across his thumb, a side effect of his pain medicine, tolmetin. At home, I rub his back, his fragile spine. Tenderly I trace each rib in the cage that protects his vital organs.

"Quit tickling me," he says.

At first I tried to make the cat into an outdoor one, but she learned to catch her paw under the door, pulling the screen away from the frame, then squeezing through the space. Before I knew she was pregnant, I was grudgingly resigned to the litter box smell and cat hair all over the furniture. Now I'm excited instead. The cat's pregnancy gives me a sense of purpose here in this small town where there is nothing for me to do, where I keep applying for jobs but nothing comes of my applications. Now I'm needed. The cat needs me. Marc needs me.

As we wait for the health insurance, while Marc distracts himself with the garden, I occupy myself with the cat, taking care of her almost as if she's a child, solicitous about her food and litter, only reluctantly disturbing her when she's sleeping. I hesitate to make the bed, shifting the layers of the cat's earth. Curled at the end of the bed, she whimpers in her sleep as I gingerly pull up the sheet, then the blanket, then the quilt. The cat wakes, rises, stumbles across the sliding covers to the floor.

Later that day as the sky darkens with an oncoming storm, Marc and I head to Safeway to buy seeds. "I'm an old man," he says gloomily. "Even if I don't have cancer, I'll be dead in ten years. This is as far as I can lift my arm." He holds it straight out in front of him, then aligns it with my arm. He obtains great self-satisfaction from comparing my pale limbs to his darker ones.

We duck out of the rain into the store for groceries. Shopping makes me tense. Given his salary and the hospital bills we may soon face, the way Marc tosses packages of chicken and steak into the cart seems extravagant. He's the one making the money, though, so I don't say anything.

On the way home, columns of rain form on the grimy windows. He rolls down his and cold, moist air blows through the cab.

"I wish you wouldn't talk about dying," I say.

Out the window, he raises his arm as high as he can, parallel with his shoulder, then lets it drop. "Lifting the wind is like lifting twenty pounds," he says, as if to reassure me that he's still taking care of himself. His arm sways from side to side, but not up and down, because it can't.

At home he lies down. He asks if I will rub his back, but that proves too painful. I massage his legs instead, reminding myself that the disease was there before I met him. That it's not my fault.

The cat settles between us on the bed and goes to sleep.

"I have a story for you to write," Marc says. "About a person constrained by a handicap or disease in a physically demanding job, afraid he won't ever succeed, hating himself and his body as a result."

"I think that's your story to write." I work my way to his toes, gently bending them forward. I wonder what the lesser of the evils is: cancer, or this daily pain as he lugs around his camera bag, rushing to fires and car accidents, on his feet much of the day. I bend his toes back, forward, back. There are no good answers.

"Crack them," Marc says.

"That's gross," I respond, and set to work softening the tough skin of his heel.

The next day he begins writing a story he never finishes. He's mostly given up carpentry, and now his photographer job is taking its toll. "I have terrible genes. I am the precursor. It will all come out in the next generation," Marc says gloomily. It's as if he sees himself as some sort of monster. I sympathize. Ever since eighth grade, I've seen myself as secretly hideously abnormal. But I also wonder, Since Marc is not a monster, does that mean that I'm not, either?

He lies flat on his stomach, arms sprawled under his head, waiting for a back rub. "Tell me a story," he says. "Something that makes you really mad." I list everything I can think that irritates me, people who pass on the right, people who treat women like they're automatically stupid. Marc drowses, coming alert only to say "harder!" or "higher!" before sinking again.

I fill him in on gossip in letters from family and friends. He mutters something into the pillow and I squeeze muscles, pound his spine, and work the small of his back. My own back is starting to hurt as I balance on the shifting mattress.

"Mmm," he says occasionally. "Mmm." He practically purrs like the cat. His eyes are closed and he has a goofy smile on his face. I'm pretty sure he's no longer listening.

"And then I got pregnant with triplets and murdered their father with an ax," I say. "When the babies were born, I drowned them."

"Mmm," he says.

June–September 1984

The possibility of cancer hangs over us, unspoken, each evening as we tour his garden, me nodding at his observations. The watermelon plant is growing a second set of leaves. Bugs have left the radish leaves more hole than leaf, like uneven little green screens. The corn leans too far to the west. Marc thinks maybe he should stake up the stalks.

"They aren't very strong," he says.

He wakes me on a Sunday morning two weeks later, cupping radishes in his hands. "Our first produce," he announces. "We each have to take a bite."

"I hate radishes," I say sleepily.

"So do I." He takes one bite anyway and holds it out to me. After that I can't sleep because of the heat in my mouth.

I'm desperate to get a job and bring in some money. I call about every employment ad that seems within the realm of possibility. "Do you have children?" asks a man in response to my inquiry about a secretarial position. "Women with children are unreliable." I don't think employers are supposed to say things like that, or write in their ads, "No women with family hangups." Marc grunts supportively when I tell him that I'm skipping those ads.

My car is broken and there's no money to fix it, so I walk everywhere. One day I walk thirteen blocks in 100-degree heat to interview for a secretary job, arriving hoarse, slick with sweat, and sagging with exhaustion. The next week I go to interview for a salesperson position for a tiny Fotomat on the edge of a parking lot. There I find a snaking line of housewives waiting their turns to be interviewed for ten minutes each in the passenger seat of a car.

And then my mom calls with news. She'd bought us a major medical insurance policy when we first got married, and it's still in effect. It will cover Marc's tests.

What if he's not sick? I wonder. Will we be back to square one, only a matter of time before we return to deciding the future of our marriage? These last few weeks, the possibility of cancer has been a reprieve from that. When I acknowledge that, is it akin to wishing him to be ill?

Just as we're sitting down to dinner, there's a rap at the door. The woman on the porch introduces herself to me as Agnes, the *Pratt Tribune* receptionist. She's carrying a little black bag that reminds me of toy doctor kits, the ones that come with a plastic stethoscope and thermometer and a vial of candy pills.

"I have the gift of healing," she says. She's a big-boned woman with small black-framed glasses and black hair that swings like a curtain to veil half her face.

"I told her to stop by," Marc tells me. He has thrown on some blue scrubs he wears as pajamas and is towel-drying his hair while Agnes makes the circuit of the living room common to first-time visitors, jumping back startled by the painting on the wall of a woman wearing a dirty shawl that hangs around her face and enfolds her thin, bent shoulders. It's her accusing stare that freaks people out, the way her chin juts angrily to one side. "Did you paint that?" Agnes asks Marc.

"My mom did," Marc says. "From a picture in *National Geographic*."

She pauses at the spinning wheel in the corner. She turns to me, hovering awkwardly in the doorway. "Oh, do you spin?" she asks.

"Oh, no, I used to," Marc says. "I haven't in a while, but someday I want to try spinning all of this hair that our dog sheds."

Agnes comments on the healthy plants in the window, the stereo in the corner, the many records, the shelf, the couch. Marc's the one with the green thumb. It's his stereo, his music collection. He built the shelf. His mother re-covered the couch. I'm embarrassed. It doesn't look like I live here at all.

I go back to my meal in the kitchen, which is only divided from the living room by the line between carpet and linoleum. "I'll eat in a while," Marc says.

Agnes tells Marc to remove his shirt and lie face down on the floor. Then she stands a candle on his back, lights it, and centers a glass over it. The flame sputters out and the circle of skin under the glass turns red and swells. I have a vague feeling that Agnes has overstepped some boundary, but Marc doesn't seem uncomfortable. In fact, he sighs and groans and I find myself bristling, growing prickly. I turn my back and finish my supper.

Agnes talks about feet. Each part of the foot is connected to another part of the body, she says.

She rifles through her black bag and produces a crumpled chart. It maps out where various parts of the feet link to eyes and lungs and pancreas and small intestine. Thoughtfully, she presses along the base of his toes, pausing at his middle one.

"You have an ear problem?"

"How did you know?"

I'm sure he must have mentioned his ear infection at work.

But she doesn't mention cancer. Maybe there is no cancer.

"Agnes gave me an amazing back rub," he tells me later.

"I think she's trying to come between us," I answer.

"Oh, no," he replies. "We're just friends. You're my wife. Don't you know how important you are to me?"

How long, I wonder, will I be important to him if he doesn't have cancer?

The next day, I offer Marc a backrub. "Gentle," he says. "My back's really sore."

I think about Agnes's chart showing how everything is connected as I rub his legs and then his feet, kneading the centers, imagining that will somehow soothe his back.

"Harder," Marc says. I think about Agnes. I punch his foot and wonder if he's attracted to her.

"Do I give good rubs?" I ask.

"You're about the best," he answers sleepily.

"About? Who's better?"

"My sister's pretty good. She's not as gentle as you are."

"But she's better?"

"Maybe a little."

"What about Agnes?"

"She's really good too."

I move up his back. I pound it with my fists and knead the muscles hard.

"Ow." He flinches away. "That's a sore spot. Be careful."

My hands drift down his back, then return to squeeze the sore spot.

"Ow!" Marc leaps up. "I told you that hurt!"

I shift my gaze from the pained, wary look in his eyes to my hands that wanted to hurt him.

"Why did you do that?" he asks.

"I'm sorry. Here. I'll be careful."

He leans against the couch, assessing me as if he will never trust me enough to turn his back on me again.

"Please?"

Slowly, he lowers himself to the carpet. I gently massage his back, even loosen the tense muscles in his neck, knowing that I can never reverse the damages that quietly pile up, my secret betrayals: my avoidance of sex, my fantasies about Cole, my own ambivalence about our marriage and about the possibility of cancer.

All the way to Wichita, to the hospital, Marc holds my hand. His mother has dressed up for the occasion: rayon pantsuit, low black pumps, a tastefully faint scent of lilacs. Dark circles, left over from her recent eye job, raccoon her eyes.

Marc and I both have on T-shirts, me with jeans, him with raggedy cutoffs and flip-flops. "You're wearing that?" Evelyn asks him as if we are getting ready to go to a fancy dinner.

In the hospital room, I tie Marc's green hospital gown while Evelyn politely averts her eyes. She and I sit together in the waiting room while Marc is in surgery. She works on a needlepoint project while I try to concentrate on my Bible lesson. Once I asked Evelyn to teach me how to cross-stitch, but I got bored quickly and the tiny squares strained my eyes. We don't connect at all. I try to recommend books to her, but she frowns at my shelves crammed with paperbacks and says, with a hint of disapproval, "I guess I'm just very selective about what I read."

A TV suspended near the ceiling drones. Evelyn glances up every now and then as she stitches Xs. It awes me how the Xs accumulate, start to look like a garden of flowers. I used to think you could plan out your life and then carefully follow a path, a pattern, one moment after another to get to where you wanted to go. But now it's all seeming to me more haphazard than the careful stitches on Evelyn's cloth, one small moment, one small decision at a time, the pattern only visible in retrospect. Her stitches are so assured. Her hands fumble but her thread never tangles and her stitches never become loose and sloppy like mine.

I leaf through my Bible study notebook. Marriage, the notes remind me, is God's sacred purpose. He hates divorce. According to Matthew, it's adultery to divorce and remarry. Luke takes it a step further—it's adultery to marry anyone who's divorced. Corinthians says that any wife who splits from her husband needs to remain single, and Matthew identifies several kinds of people who God has destined for singleness—for instance, the commentary explains, some people are born with a disability that makes sexual intercourse impossible.

I freeze. I've never heard of ambiguous genitalia or other biological anomalies, and I think this is about people like me. Maybe God has given me this terrible disability, made sex wrenchingly painful, in order to force me to stay single. Have I thwarted God's plan by marrying Marc, displeased Him by ignoring His will?

I close my notebook. I'm not sure I can accept a God this cruel and harsh, one who purposely creates human beings incapable of being loved, one who would make it a sin for me to marry again if Marc leaves me.

Evelyn stares down with her bruised eyes as she whips her needle in and out of cloth, making expert stitches. *The New Newlywed Game* plays on the suspended TV.

"When he's behind the wheel of the Lovemobile," Bob Eubanks asks the wives, "do you most often tell him to speed up or slow down?"

The wives seem to think the question is about driving. The men think it's about sex.

I blush. Evelyn remains pleasantly opaque.

The doctor beckons from the hall. I leap up, Evelyn in tow.

"The spot I saw on the X-ray was gone," the doctor says. Evelyn and I avoid looking at each other, but I can feel her relief. I tamp down any hint of regret.

Marc's painkiller is causing his stomach to bleed. The spot likely was a blood clot, not a tumor.

"How often do you have sex?" the doctor asks me, point-blank right there in front of Evelyn. I blush fiercely.

"We'd been living apart," I say. "And then we were worried."

"There was quite a buildup of semen," the doctor says. "You should have more sex."

In retrospect, this comment will rankle: surrounding me are messages that sex is something that a wife owes her husband, that my own difficulties are irrelevant. Someday, after the marriage ends, I will make more conscious choices, finding boyfriends who are considerate and solicitous. Maybe, unbeknownst to me, the endometriosis I wasn't aware of will go into remission. At any rate, those difficulties will completely disappear, leaving me perplexed by the mysteries of the body, never sure why pain was such an issue in my relationship with Marc.

But for now, when Marc wakes, I'm at his bedside, and we make light of the doctor's advice. What now? I wonder, secretly. Now what will become of our marriage?

After I've been around Marc's mother or his brother and sister for a few days, I feel drained, exhausted, unable to speak. I'm pretty sure his family thinks I'm autistic. He's impatient at the way I check out; it will be years before I realize that there's nothing especially pathological or even atypical about this: I'm just an introvert and need time to myself. Home again, I feel as if I'm slowly reinhabiting my body, my life.

Kitty delivers her litter in the closet in my basement study. Then she moves her kittens upstairs to the space between the wall and the bed, four black kittens with Siamese meows, eyes still tightly shut. Gradually, the babies turn fat and open their wide blue eyes. The garden is an expanse of green textures, blades poking up through soil, smooth green stalks with pointy and feathery and wide leaves that create dark shady spots. The kittens tumble through all that green, batting at plants swaying in the breeze.

We confine the kittens to the basement, which they plunder. Allowed back upstairs, they pull down the door screen and poke their heads through the holes in the center of 45s. They climb the insides of the curtain so that it bulges and recedes like an outgoing tide. I'm lying on the floor wiggling a string in front of one when another playfully claws at Marc. His hand whips into the air. Something soft on the surface, hard underneath, hits my face, and a small body thuds against the floor. The kitten leaps and runs away.

Marc's anger is building again, he's starting to withdraw again, wincing again at too much company or attention.

And suddenly what I fear most is not that he'll leave me, but that someday, I'll have had enough. That someday, if this continues, I'll withdraw, stop trying to be a good wife. Already, sometimes, I watch the way other men lounge in chairs and lope down streets and I wonder what it would be like to be with someone so at ease in his own skin.

To look behind him, Marc turns his whole body. Sometimes he has to climb on a stool to reach high shelves since he can't lift his arm. I don't remember him doing any of this before our marriage, and so my guilt triples—for causing his disease to progress, for blaming him instead of myself for our almost complete moratorium on sex, and for my longing for other men.

When Marc complains about his job, where he works sixty hours a week but barely makes enough for us to scrape by, I say, "What would you rather do?"

"With this fucked-up body?" he asks, and refuses to answer. He still has rashes and blood in his urine. His doctor has ordered him to stop taking tolmetin, which is too hard on his stomach, but there is nothing less harsh to replace it.

I have found homes for all of the kittens, and at first I think that Kitty is unhappy with me about that, since she is always following me, meowing plaintively. She seems tormented. I'll hear her on the porch, in the side yard, her loud, nasal yowling. I pick her up and, dismayed, realize that her sides are bulging again.

"She's really getting annoying," Marc says.

"She's getting so skinny," I say. It doesn't make any sense. Even though she appears to be pregnant and ravenously devours everything, she is losing weight. The other night we left the dinner table when two cars collided in front of our house. By the time we returned, Kitty had licked all the spaghetti clean. There was no trace of sauce.

I walk into the kitchen as Marc pushes Kitty off the counter. "She's acting starved," he says. "Getting into everything."

"Be careful," I say as Kitty dashes under the couch.

We should have had her fixed, I keep thinking. I should have cut back on groceries or something so that we could afford to have her fixed.

When I get the mail, when the cat streaks by me and into the house, I'm daydreaming about tracking down my college Spanish professor and running off with him. I balance on the edge of the bed to sort mail, and when I lift my hand, it's covered in blood.

I stare uncomprehendingly at the wet red stain on the quilt. Wadding up the quilt, I throw it into the laundry basket before I notice the trail of blood across the kitchen floor.

With her claws, the cat pulls on the throw rug by the door. Her eyes are clouded. She labors to her feet, leaving another spot.

All of a sudden, she tears off toward the bedroom, watery blood spattering. She leaps onto the bed and burrows under the covers. I fling back the blanket. She jumps to the floor and races off.

She has miscarried on the sheet.

My stomach turns at the sight of those blobs of tissue, half-formed kittens. I hasten to clean them up and start the washing machine.

Stroking the cat, rubbing the damp pads of her paws, I remember all the times Marc pushed her off of the counter. I want to cast blame. I want him to be at fault. I walk around feeling angry even though I know that sometimes things just happen.

Marc retains his enthusiasm for gardening for a few weeks. He makes pickles from the first cucumbers, complaining about spending all that time for three measly jars. He worries over the leaning cornstalks until he is convinced that they will never yield good corn, and after that, he ignores them. The watermelon seems dry, and the pot of green beans he cooked doesn't taste quite right. He finally stops thrusting tomatoes on the neighbors. Everyone already has too many tomatoes.

He talks about making ketchup, but then a front comes in and he's too sore. He's so stiff that he finally just lets the garden go. I rub his back, even trying to crack his toes to distract him.

In September, one of his coworkers suggests that Kitty might have worms. I crush worm pills and mix them with her food. She starts to recover immediately, gaining weight, her tortured yowls fading. I begin a part-time job working for a tax accountant, spending mornings typing tax forms and sorting checks, deposit slips, and receipts for clients. With my first paycheck, we have the cat spayed.

"What's your cat's name?" the veterinary assistant asks me.

"Um—Kitty?" I say, embarrassed that we've never properly named her.

"Lots of people name their cats Kitty," she reassures me.

"The landlord wants us to clean up the garden," Marc says. "Can you do it?" He seems far away, polite, unnaturally formal. "Have you ever thought about what it would be like to be blind and want to paint pictures?" he asks gloomily.

Before I go out to take care of the garden, there's something I need to do. I go down to the basement to my office tucked way at the very back. I empty a bookshelf and carry it upstairs. Then I haul up piles of books. I build a wall of bookshelves between the kitchen and the living room. Now, when anyone walks through the door, the first thing they'll see, before the painting or spinning wheel or plants or stereo, is my books.

With her shaved belly, Kitty plays Jungle Cat in the overgrown garden. She races out and crouches down in the grass as I approach. Bracing myself against brittle cornstalks, I jolt backward as they pull free from the dirt. Pretending to be a shadow, Kitty lies in the shadow of a tomato plant. A robin lands and she leaps. The bird beats its wings and shrieks as she sinks her teeth into its fat belly and parades it upside down along the garden's borders. Lately she keeps coming into the house with feathers stuck to her mouth or leaves butterfly wings in neat piles by her food dish. Good health has brought out the predator in her.

As I toss cornstalks into a pile, corncobs roll in the dirt. Worms have picked all the kernels clean. I pull up radishes the size and shape of fists, clear away tomatoes that explode at a touch. The cucumbers are soft and yellow, like bananas. Weeds have choked out green beans and onions. I kneel to pull up carrots, yank too hard, and nearly fall backward when a carrot comes loose from the dirt.

I expect it to be long and thin and useless, like the first one I picked in July, but these are as big as carrots from Safeway. It seems miraculous, these intact carrots in the neglected garden.

I break off the end of one and chew it. Even flavored by dirt, it tastes unmistakably like a carrot. I feel like Scarlett O'Hara, shaking her fist at the sky. "As God is my witness," I think. "As God is my witness, I'll never be hungry again."

Flinging the carrot down, I hurry along the row, piling up vegetables, salvaging this one small thing from the fear and blame and guilt and neglect and decay of the summer, not even pausing to wipe my dirt-encrusted hands on my jeans. I fold up my shirt hem and fill it with carrots, imagining that when Marc comes home he will find them, cleaned and peeled, stacked by the sink. That we will eat them with our dinner while the cat lies plumped out like a laying hen in the dying sunlight, while Marc puts aside his restlessness for one more night. That we will savor the taste of what survives.

Pillow put out

Firefighter Jim Zeltner uses a garden hose to douse a smoldering pillow that caught fire at 702 S. Hamilton Sunday. Berkly Miller, Pratt fire chief, said the pillow ignited because it was stored on top of a water heater.

FLIGHT: PART 1
Pratt, Kansas

Fall 1984

AT 2:00 A.M., I wake to thunder that rattles the house. A flash of lightning reveals Marc's creased cheek, his sleeping face. Suddenly, the mattress shifts as he sits up. "I'm going to go take pictures," he says.

I hear him gather his camera bag before the door slams. He goes out whenever there's a storm. I imagine him on a hill somewhere, camera poised, waiting for lightning to call up a skyline of chimneys and silos.

Sometimes I imagine some other woman having a lover who comes to her only during storms. I'm not as bothered by that idea as I ought to be. One day recently I found Marc in the kitchen, cooking lunch, a red ring on his white athletic sock like a lipstick kiss. He'd dropped a Ro-tel tomato, he said, and it was true, those canned tomatoes could easily slip right out of your grip and skitter across the floor, and I laughed sheepishly: What, Marc was cheating on me with a lipsticked woman who liked to kiss his sock?

Now, the storm riles up, crashing and flashing, rain pounding, then gradually dies down to brief rumbles of far-off thunder, rain dripping from the eaves. Half asleep when Marc returns, I feel to check if his hair is damp. It is, and his skin is cold, and tomorrow he will develop lightning photos, his alibi. He puts his cold feet on my calves and snuggles against me, immediately drifting off to sleep.

As it gets colder out, I've taken to trailing my fingers along the light switches, feeling static tingle across my fingertips, then brushing my hand against the back of his neck. It's a weird kind of satisfaction, this small pain I pass to him. Sometimes I wish he was having an affair, if that would make him less tense and angry, make him contrite and sad instead. We are always stressed by our different approaches to life. Not just because he, an extrovert, finds my need to be alone to recharge to be pathological, but because he prefers spontaneity, independence, and freedom while I'm far more comfortable with advance planning and expect compromise and consultation when it comes to decisions.

I've always known that our families are radically different, his passive-aggressive, thriving on small talk, mine more direct but reticent, reluctant to waste words. But I've always thought our commonalities might make up for the differences in our backgrounds, the fact that we both grew up in Wichita, home of an airport, four airplane plants, and an Air Force base. Planes were always passing low over the highway, suspending conversations and lessons, knocking countless stories off track, leading to untold amounts of lost information.

I used to cultivate friendships full of talk and confidences, but marriage, like a low-flying plane, has changed me. I'm not sure how to start conversations about my sense that I'm in the wrong life. It's easier to give up, to retreat into silence or meaningless small talk. It's like over the years the thundering backdrop of airplanes has finally defeated me, rousing tiny hairs in my ears that continue to vibrate, so that between planes, they ring, a small, continuous tinniness that drowns out everything I've thought of saying.

Sometimes I'm mad at myself for deferring graduate school to move here to Pratt for him. We had no idea how overworked he would be, or how hard it would be for me to find work at all before I finally start my part-time morning job as an accountant's assistant. It's not what I want to do with my life, but it's fine for now, and I hope that our marriage will find a comfortable rhythm.

But often Marc seems distant, frustrated. I'll come home to find the living room thumping with music, camera bag toppled on the couch, Marc working in the basement on his clip file.

I sneak up behind him and touch his neck, transferring a shock to him.

Sometimes when I do this, he laughs, but this time he flinches and says, "Stop that."

Strips of paper fly as he razors out another picture.

"I feel so trapped," he says. "I hate this job. I wish I could be free of everything that's restricting me."

I'm pretty sure he doesn't just mean the job. I'm pretty sure he also means our marriage.

When I head to the library to apply for a card and inquire about jobs, Marc calls after me, "Don't hold your breath." Once he witnessed a librarian giving a tour to schoolchildren, pointing out a book in a glass case. "We used to leave this book out but people were reading it all the time and we had to lock it up," she'd said, or so Marc swears, convinced that the librarian sees books as artifacts to be preserved rather than items to be read. Another time, he claims, a girl ahead of him in line at the reference desk asked to look at Kansas statutes. The clerk refused. "You wouldn't understand them," she'd said. "Only a lawyer could understand them."

The woman at the desk impatiently shakes her head when I ask about job openings, but my request for a card meets with more success. She winds a paper into the typewriter and says, "What's your husband's name?"

Mystified, I answer, then with growing trepidation, watch her tap out letters. Sure enough, she's issuing me a card under Marc's name. Suddenly, my name is Mrs. Marc.

After an evening of stewing, I return. "This isn't my name," I stammer. "I want my name on the card." Puzzled and a little hostile, she makes me a new card.

Marc commiserates. Whenever he asks for photo identifications, women tend to give him their husbands' names instead of their own.

So I go on typing tax forms in the mornings, and the rest of the time, I take care of the cat and the dog and read books. We don't have any TV reception and can't afford cable, and long-distance phone calls are too expensive, so

I eagerly await the mail and the newspaper for contact with the outside world. The newspaper Marc works for reports mostly local events: how a size-six Stride Rite shoe is found on Main Street after a parade, how a firefighter is called to douse a smoldering pillow, ignited when stored on top of a water heater. Marc is sent to photograph the pillow, which is still emitting trails of smoke on someone's front lawn.

> **Found**
> Following the Centennial Parade, one white, child's size 6D Stride Rite shoe was taken to the law enforcement center.

Sometimes, I think, we're sort of happy. There's something comforting about the companionship of marriage. I wake many mornings with a sense of well-being and experience moments of joy. Marc and I laugh a lot. There are good things about being together, even if there are also difficulties and frustrations. I suggest that we should cultivate more social life and we go to a party given by one of his coworkers. All of the newspaper employees gossip and exchange inside jokes. I try to appear interested even though I don't know any of them or understand the jokes or have anything to contribute to the conversation. The host gets drunk and yells at me, "Loosen up! You're making me nervous."

Finally, I slip out the front door and walk home. I'm pretty sure no one notices.

Gradually, I'm also inducted into the social life of small-town housewives. Their gatherings seem to always double as sales parties. During our time in Pratt and over the next few years in other small towns, I will go to a Tupperware party where I buy a storage container for grapes, a Mary Kay party where a lady with a pink Cadillac makes us up so that I don't recognize myself, and a purse party although I never carry a purse. I will attend a home décor party and page through a catalogue with headlines like, "Create a romantic illusion."

The sales rep offers a silk rose to the hostess. The rose, she says, represents the hostess's beauty: the petals are like her soft skin, the stem her strength, the leaves her open arms, warm touch, and willingness to serve others. We all applaud the hostess. I'm pretty sure that if the rep presented me with a rose, it would have thorns.

The rep demonstrates different arrangements of items, how you might surround a candle with fake leaves, hang a mirror behind them, and set a miniature iron park bench alongside. How you might arrange a Victorian woman statuette, which comes with a pedestal. "We always want to put women on pedestals, don't we?" the rep says. "Don't we all want to be revered and adored?"

The rep fiddles with a birdcage. "This could be a coffee table centerpiece," she says. "Or you could put a plant in it. You could even put a bird in it!" She groups candles around it. She absently sets the Victorian woman inside it, then hastily snatches her right back out.

"Oh, my," she says. "We wouldn't want to put a woman in a cage, now would we?"

On our first wedding anniversary, I try to create a romantic illusion. I buy wine, a rose, and Cornish game hens, then spend the afternoon stuffing the hens after a struggle with the giblet bags that are plastered to them by ice. I make a dinner menu, charging kisses and hugs for each item, and post a sign on the door that isn't all that romantic but I know will amuse Marc: "Nancy's a struggle with the giblet bags that are plastered to them by ice. I make a dinner menu, charging kisses and hugs for each item, and post a sign on the door that isn't all that romantic but I know will amuse Marc: "Nancy's Little Dead Chicken House." I put on Pachelbel's Canon in D and unearth leftover wedding napkins. I set out wineglasses and brass candlesticks that we received as wedding presents. When I fling a white tablecloth onto the table, it lands flat, a white athletic sock clinging to its center.

"Wow," says Marc when he gets home. "This is nice. Thank you."

I shoo him out of the room with a beer. He stretches out on the living room couch and tells me how he went up on a radio tower that morning to shoot aerial pictures of Pratt.

"That tower seemed awfully fragile when I was hanging by a cable and belt all the way up there," he says. "I had to use a higher shutter speed because I was shaking so much, I was afraid I'd blur the picture."

"I don't know if I want to hear about this." I shudder. "How was the rest of your day?"

The morning was taken up with City Council mug shots, he says. This afternoon he had to shoot a portrait of five generations of a bickering family in town for a reunion. Also, the publisher's wife assigned him a photo page on Fire Prevention Week—what is he going to take pictures of? A fire truck? A house ablaze? Another smoldering pillow? Anyway, FPW isn't in August, it's in October.

Over dinner, I try to make conversation. "So what *is* your dream job?"

He used to fantasize about being a foreign correspondent or starting his own newspaper. Lately, he's groused that traveling around Kansas as a Pixie Photographer at J.C. Penney stores would beat this job, the boring shots and the long hours cooped up in a studio developing other people's bad pictures.

"To not have to put up with this job," he says.

He stares at candlelight flickering across the heaps of bones on our plates. "I'll tell you my nightmare job," he said. "Working in a fat rendering plant. Collecting the fat off of dead animals. Think of all the maggots."

I push away my half-eaten Cornish game hen. "If you hate your job so much, we could move," I say. "You'd find something else."

His hands tense around his fork. "I'm getting lots of freelance stuff. The AP wants me to shoot a photo of an irrigation system. And did I tell you? I'm the official photographer for the Miss Kansas Pageant."

"You didn't tell me that." I start clearing the dishes. "That's kind of exciting." I dump bones into the trash. "Would you ever have an affair?" I ask.

He laughs, but then he says, "I don't think I could stand any more attention or expectations."

My stomach tightens. I've never lived on my own. I can't imagine working for an accountant for the rest of my life, but I'm not sure if there's anything I'm qualified to do to support myself. I don't know what I'll do if my marriage ends.

"Don't be paranoid," Marc says.

"People used to say I was perceptive," I answer.

I eat a cookie and drink punch in a roomful of women, coworkers of Marc's, who mention their husbands' names with possessive smiles, expressions carefully cultivated to suggest that their marriages are perfect. They make coy references from which I conclude that they have no trouble feeling attracted to their husbands and certainly have not given up on sex altogether. I doodle on my order blank and listen to other women exclaim over teddies and gowns with names like Rapture, Misty Moments, and Frilly Filly.

The sales rep announces that it's time for a game. First we each list five animals and one characteristic that describes each animal. Then we go around the room, reading our lists while the rep interprets them: the first animal, she explains, was what we're like in the morning, the second, what we're like in the evening, the third, fourth, and fifth what we're like before, during, and after sex. Most of the women have inadvertently compared themselves to cats, dogs, and elephants: they purr, slobber, and have wrinkly skin.

Before sex, my answer says, I'm like a hamster: I swallow things and spit them up.

Squeals and shrieks interrupt the game and I win a pair of lace panties for the best answer. I escape when everyone starts trying on nightgowns and putting in their orders for edible underwear. On my way home, I stuff the panties into the glove compartment.

At the Miss Kansas Pageant semi-finals, which Marc has gotten me into on his press pass, I sit at the end of the runway, watching the auditorium fill. Marc stalks around the stage, testing out different angles, his bulb flashing crazily as soon as the pageant starts and the contestants introduce themselves.

"I'm Miss Western Wheatfields," says the first. "I'm working on a degree in equestrian science at the University of Kansas, and for me that and being Miss Kansas combine into a single vision. I'm saddled up and ready to ride to Atlantic City, mount the stage, and stirrup the Miss America Pageant—but first, judges, you must give me my reign!"

Miss Scenic Flint Hills talks about her aspirations: "If I don't win this pageant," she says, "it's not like I'm going to end up destitute, in the breadlines."

I catch Marc's eye and we both repress smiles. I'm reassured by our shared appreciation of absurdity.

He grins at me again when the contestants stroll down the runway in silver and gold beaded evening gowns to "Send in the Clowns." He flashes another smile my way during the talent competition when one contestant sings "Let's Hear It for Me" from *Funny Lady* and another performs a song with the repeated line, "Please make me a winner tonight." Then he disappears backstage during the "Chattanooga Choo Choo" flute solo.

Women my age parade out in one-piece bathing suits and high heels to twirl before the judges. I'm so close to the stage that I can see them trembling at the end of the runway while an announcer tells us their height and weight and raves about what accomplished seamstresses and cooks they are. Marc's flash blinks in the wings like sudden lightning.

When the finalists are announced, I'm embarrassed at the tears in my eyes. These young women all look so happy, so hopeful. I try to remember being this hopeful ever, even on my wedding day, but I can't.

"I'm going to drop you off at home," Marc says, just when I'm imagining having tea together and rehashing the pageant. "I have to go run my film."

For the next night, the finals, the seats are all sold out and Marc can't get me in on a press pass. I find myself wishing I could watch it on TV, but when I turn on our small black-and-white set, there's only static.

"Oh, well," Marc says. "I'll take notes. I'll tell you all about it."

I let him think that I want to go so we can bond over our mutual amusement at small-town provinciality. But secretly, what I really want is to see some hopeful young woman crowned, to witness her glorious moment with a shining future spread out before her. I am twenty-one years old, and I have forgotten, if I ever knew, what that feels like.

I'm afraid that one of these days, no matter what it costs me, I'm going to have to find out.

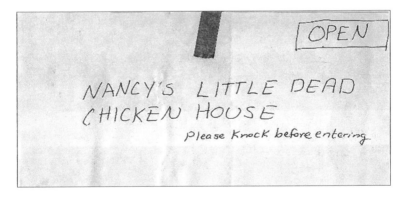

METAMORPHOSIS

ONE MORNING WHEN I was twenty-four, I woke to discover that my heart had transformed into a giant cockroach.

I was a creative writing graduate student known for the often-transparent veil between my autobiography and my fiction. Since this book is nonfiction, I feel obligated to confess: this might not have literally happened. But here are some things that are true: Cockroaches can live a week without their heads. They can live without food and water. They have been around since the time of the dinosaur. They are the most adaptable pests on earth. And I first encountered them because they infested the apartment in Arkansas that Marc and I had rented sight unseen.

The day we move to Fayetteville, we've been married for two years, and the cycle continues. Every three months, he becomes restless, moody, frustrated. Announces he doesn't want to be married. Then apologizes, brings me flowers, becomes polite and careful until the restlessness sets in again. Terror stalks me. Someday, I know, our marriage is finally going to fall apart. My family, my friends, my childhood church will all see me as a failure then, an embarrassment. I imagine facing a lonely and uncertain future. I never stop to think about whether I'm really happy. It doesn't matter. I took vows, and I take those vows seriously, and for long stretches I'm content enough.

The night before we leave for Arkansas, I dream that I'm late for the Survival of the Fittest Dance in a musical about Darwin's life. All the next day we drive, Marc's silver Toyota truck piled high with books and bedding and cast-iron pans. His brown Naugahyde chair and my orange rocker, roped on loosely, bounce on bumps. The nightstand that for years mashed my childhood carpet wobbles on curves. I follow in my orange AMC Hornet, my rear view blocked by lampshades and pillows and suitcases stuffed with clothes.

I really hate the color orange. So, apparently, do a lot of other people, which is why both the rocker and the car had been bargains. This car, with its dull finish, has a drooping ceiling so that it feels like I'm driving in a tent. My orange Hornet is the remnant of an era of lime green and sunshine yellow kitchen appliances, psychedelic multicolored shag carpet, and bell bottoms that fell like circus tents around your shoes. Sometimes it feels as if my life is populated primarily by embarrassing leftovers, outdated discards.

Marc pulls over and jogs back to where I've dutifully come to a stop on the shoulder behind him.

"Could you please not follow so close?" he says. He seems worried. "If something should fall off the truck, you could be injured."

I like this sweet and protective side of Marc. I wish he were like this all the time. Once he told me about how as a child he'd put flies in the freezer, then glued balsa wood to their wings to see what would happen when they thawed. After he told me this, I kept wondering how I could have married someone so capable of casual cruelty. But in this case, though I know he's criticizing me, I believe it comes out of his solicitous, generous impulses, and I agree to keep a couple of car lengths between us.

But getting lost seems a worse fate, so I go on tailgating.

We enter the Fayetteville city limits. Marc briskly leads us through side streets and across the University of Arkansas campus. Together we pull up in front of the married student housing and cut our motors.

Long low buildings, completely constructed of concrete, stretch out before us. A wall of latticed stonework surrounds each building so that no windows are visible. Heaps of ragged shingles litter the sidewalk, their tarry smell overpowering in the heat. Shirts and nightgowns draped over balconies gesture their arms sluggishly in a mild breeze.

Earlier today, Marc and I left his mother's house in a neighborhood with green lawns and redwood decks, shuttered windows and backyard grills where we'd lived, in limbo and with no privacy, for five months. Back in Pratt, the last time he'd announced that he didn't think we should have gotten married, I decided that I was leaving. I told him that I was going to go to graduate school, and he could come or not. To my surprise and relief, he not only agreed to come, he used the plan as an excuse to quit his job then and there, and that's how we'd ended up at his mom's, saving money for the move to Arkansas. His mother's quiet, tasteful street seems a world away from these windowless, medievally modernistic buildings squatting on scraggly brownish grass.

Slowly, Marc climbs out of his truck and trudges over to my Hornet, where I remain immobilized by horror.

"They're putting in a new roof," he observes in a way-too-chipper tone. "That's a good sign."

"I want to go home," I say.

"You must really hate it if you want to go back to my mother's," he replies.

This is true. I'd tiptoed around his mother's house, afraid to leave my book on the coffee table or my shoes by the couch or my laundry in the dryer, knowing that everything would be scooped up and deposited in the guest room within the hour, a constant reminder that this was not our home. I'd rinsed every dish after finishing with it, hung my towel immediately after showering, said nothing when Marc's mother brought home dinner for herself and Marc but none for me.

Marc had felt far more free to scatter his stuff around the house, since he was gone for hours every day, busy building a cabin on his uncle's property on the Ninnescah River. His mother considered this valid work, unlike my office jobs. She'd frowned at the books I read and whatever I ate or wore. And she'd really disliked Kitty, who was freaked out at being uprooted, eventually running out the front door and never returning. For weeks, feeling displaced and constricted, I'd searched the lawns and streets for some sign of our cat.

Now, I'm pretty sure that I'd rather live in a dungeon with rats than with his mother ever again, so I buck up and get out of the car, hoping that the inside of our new apartment will be more appealing than the outside.

My whole life, it seems, I've been longing for change, for some defining moment when my real life can begin. My ugly orange rocker was a manifestation of that yearning: at thirteen, edgy, agitated, embarrassed by my pink-carpeted, rose-wallpapered bedroom, I set out to diffuse its girly sweetness and innocence. The orange chair was on sale, and though it clashed aggressively with pink, I was looking for a fight. I didn't realize that the color scheme of my bedroom would come to feel like a tug of war for my soul, an opposition between two colors I didn't want to identify with.

Now as we lug boxes into this apartment that fails after all to pleasantly surprise me, I even miss my old pink bedroom while Marc tries to reassure me. "We don't have to stay here," he says. "As soon as I find a job, we'll move." He's being unusually patient.

Our new place is cramped and dark. There's an efficiency kitchen on one wall, a tiny bathroom, and two closet-sized bedrooms barely big enough to fit a mattress. The walls are concrete blocks and the floors terra cotta, which sounded, in the apartment description, vaguely indigenous, like clay stomped into place by native tribes. Instead, it turns out, terra cotta is a fancy name for yet more concrete, this time a brownish-orange color. There is so much concrete, you could install drains and take a shower anywhere.

Together, Marc and I haul in our kitchen table and wooden chairs, the recliner and rocker, some lawn chairs and TV trays. I rest for a second in my hideous orange rocker, trying to calm my racing thoughts. I have read and rocked in this chair for years, rocked so vigorously that twice the seat flew off the base, propelling me into the air, landing across the room with a teeth-rattling thud. My dad hammered the chair back together both times.

Now, I find myself rocking hard as if that will soothe the panic that won't die down. The once-comforting motion sends the chair scooting backward over the bare floor. It's impossible to rock and stay in one place.

I'm regretting my decision to move here for graduate school. The official story has always been that I deferred entrance for a year because of Marc's job in Pratt, but in reality I was secretly terrified at the idea that I'd have to teach to put myself through, I, who always blushed and went speechless when called on in class. Now, looking around this apartment, I feel only dread and regret: What have I done, moving our whole lives here?

While Marc piles more boxes in the kitchen area, I set to work cleaning. Not even hot water and steel wool will budge the orange pool of sticky goo in the kitchen cabinet. Grease streaks the oven door. A cobweb in the bathroom catches in my hair and tickles my cheek. The walls appear clean, but I soap them down and wipe them with hot water. I scrub the clean refrigerator as dusk falls like more dirt sifting into the room.

I slice cheese and butter bread. We sit at the table to eat our grilled cheese sandwiches, such a tranquil, ordinary ritual. Marc says that he's going to start looking for a job right away, and then we'll move. For now, we'll get a scrap of carpet to make it more homey and keep my chair from skittering across the floor.

Everything will be all right, I think, my dismay subsiding for the first time in hours.

Then I look up to see a brown bug on the wall, twitching its antennae. I scream.

Marc chases after it, but right before his crumpled napkin can close over the bug, it races along the seam between two blocks, right toward me. I leap from the table, screaming.

Marc raises his eyebrows, bemused by this new side of me. The bug has come to a standstill. Only its antennae, thin as hairs, tremble. Then it plops to the floor.

Marc lunges after it. It darts through a crack in the wall.

"I want to go home," I say. So much for dungeons and rats.

"It's just one bug," Marc insists. "It probably just wandered in from outside."

I throw away my sandwich, wash my plate. My appetite is gone.

When I was little and wished for more friends, my dad always said, "You can catch more flies with honey than with vinegar." But the nicer I was, the more people dismissed me as too quiet and not very smart. I hope that going to graduate school will be different, once I meet people with whom I have more in common. And besides, I think sometimes, why would I want to catch flies anyway?

After our months of limbo, I've been imagining this move to Arkansas as the point at which my life will really begin. Never mind that past attempts to reinvent myself have mostly gone awry.

Take when I was fifteen and resolved to return to school at the end of the summer with a new haircut, wardrobe, contacts, a tan, a job, a driver's license, maybe even a boyfriend. Gradually, each ambition fell flat, knocked over one after another like a row of dominoes. I was bored lying in the sun, my hair, once cropped short, waved wildly in opposite directions, I got repeatedly lost as a candy striper wheeling sagging sick patients to occupational and physical therapy. Contacts burned my eyes and six weeks of driver's ed resulted in a temporary license and a paralyzing terror of mixing up the gas and brake pedals.

While I had long ago abandoned my home-sewn, double-knit polyester pantsuits and too-short jeans that my mom had lengthened by adding colorful strips of cloth to their bell bottoms, my wardrobe still consisted largely of home-made turtleneck T-shirts.

My mom and I had no idea how to actually shop for clothes. We wandered stores like immigrants from Pluto, staring with bewilderment at all the choices, the colors and patterns and styles and accessories, so overwhelmed that we finally spun around and left.

And then, worst of all, when I followed the lead of my friends and tried to call Cole, then just a long-standing crush, he wasn't home. I threw down the receiver, leaving a moist circle where my palm had gripped it, sure that nothing would ever change.

I hadn't rushed into marriage at twenty so much as sleepwalked, another floundering attempt to reinvent my life, to find some safety in a dangerous world, to find some certainty in an uncertain one. The semester following our wedding, I took a poetry class in which I wrote deeply disillusioned pieces full of jaded observations. My classmates concluded that I'd been married at least thirty years.

The morning after our arrival in Fayetteville, Marc goes off job hunting and I tuck myself into my orange chair to write. I'm working on a story about two kids in love, based on me and Cole. In my story, the girl and boy are meant for each other, but are so shy they can't get up the courage to kiss. At their favorite diner, the girl orders her customary carrot cake with cream cheese frosting. The waitress serves her an extra big piece and shakes her head at the boy. "That little girl of yours needs to eat more or she's just going to waste away," she says.

In the car, the boy and girl hint around a lot and stare at each other. Finally, too terrified to make the first move, she slides out and crosses the dark to the porch. Behind her, his car backs out to the street, slowly, slowly, idling, a crunch of gravel, a rush backward, a puff of air. Her longing for her life to turn a corner, her hope dissolving in puffs of air.

It turns out that the average infested household contains more than twenty thousand roaches. Divide that among the ten or so units in our building, and only about two thousand reside in ours.

Bugs come out of spaces I didn't know were there, gaps between bricks, the crack between the wall and door-frame, the dark crevice where the cabinet is affixed to the wall, every breach and chink, slit and slot, vent and cranny that usually exist outside of human awareness. Bugs dart out, exposing fractures, refusing to remain relegated to subconsciousness.

At first, it's one bug crawling on the wall, two circling the bathroom sink, three zipping out of a box of pots and pans that remains unopened since there's nowhere to store its contents. A bug escapes from a drawer where I keep stamps. It's been nourishing itself on the glue. I make frequent trips to Walmart's Household Pests section, stocking an arsenal of Raid and Roach Motels. I blast roaches with the faucet until they wash down the drain, frantically paddling their little legs. I store my toothbrush in the fridge's butter dish to keep it safe. My skin crawls with tactile hallucinations: tiny feet shiver across my arms and I slap at breezes in my hair. At night I skim the surface of sleep and wake shuddering, unable to distinguish, in that post-dream foggy state, the difference between dreams and roaches. Both are slippery, thick-shelled, weaving in and out of darkness, taking on symbolic meaning greater than the sum of their parts. I'm afraid to get up to pee. I fear the whole floor shifting when I turn on the light, a solid layer of roaches scuttling for darkness.

My muscles hurt, achy from being tensed all the time. I start when sunlight filtered through the concrete grill turns to shifting freckles across the floor. Adrenaline dizzies me at the swinging shadow of a shoestring on the tiles, the movement of my reflected hand in the TV tray's aluminum edge. I stalk a bug on the carpet. I bat at it with a shoe but miss. The bug bounces in the air, its legs still scrabbling, and lands. I bat again. The bug bounces again and again hits the ground running. We go on like that, as if the bug is a small basketball that I am dribbling across the scrap of carpet.

Within a few hours after I set out the Roach Motels, sixteen check in and remain, caught in motion, frozen in lifelike poses like Pompeii victims under ash. A roach wanders into a Motel and out again, finding no vacancies, wading over the stepping-stones of its cousins' corpses. I deluge the emerging bug with Raid until it's shiny, burnished to a high gloss. It skitters like a weak-ankled child on ice skates. It staggers, its antennae quiver and fold, and, in a dramatic death scene worthy of Shakespeare, it keels over on its back.

After moving unpacked boxes to a storage unit where I hope that any errant bugs will starve, we escape for the weekend to my parents' ramshackle vacation house on Table Rock Lake in Missouri. My parents and aunts and uncles and cousins ask me if I'm ready to go back to school. My parents are proud that I've received full funding, so I just smile and fake nonchalance.

We ride around on my dad's secondhand speedboat, and I hear Marc telling my cousins about his childhood torture of flies. How he caught them in his bare hands, how they'd tickle inside his fist. How he'd take them out of the freezer and glue wood to their wings. Thawing, those little fly planes lifted, circled the room, then sluggish from the weight, crashed to the carpet, dead on impact. Marc's hands swoop, lag, loop toward the floor as they impersonate flies. My cousins laugh. I join them uneasily, newly aware of my own capacity for small acts of violence.

Marc takes a few turns on the skis, gracefully skimming the water as my cousins cheer. "You want to try?" he asks me.

I don't. But everyone is looking at me expectantly. I crawl over the side of the boat, resigned. I follow Marc's directions as I strap on the skis. "Get in a fetal position," Marc says, and I bend my knees like a fetus floating in amniotic fluid, feeling weirdly helpless. "Yeah, like that. Cannonball position." I clasp my knees to my chest tight, powerful, ready to explode. I straighten my arms.

The boat lunges forward, gradually pulling me up to a squat. It takes a few tries, but finally I rise all the way to my feet, leaning back, gliding over water, over the bumps created by the boat's wake. I, who took Interpersonal Communication so I didn't have to take Public Speaking in college, I, who will soon stand before twenty-two freshmen, am standing on water, slicing through it. My skis tip up before me like bug antennae. I am powerful, indestructible. I can walk on water, I can do this, I think right before I topple over, slamming into the water in a tangle of limbs and skis.

It turns out that I love new TA orientation, meeting so many people I click with, people who like to talk about books and writing and yes, even grammar. Over lunch the first day, my new friends, all single, are astonished to learn that I'm married.

"Two years," I say, as if I am leading a normal life, as if we're happy.

Later in the week, they briefly meet Marc. "You seem like such good friends," they say.

"We are," I reply. I can't explain that that's what we've evolved into: good friends in a sexless marriage.

I'm giddy with happiness at having all of these potential friends, until the moment that a roach meanders out of my purse and crawls across the classroom floor while all of my new colleagues, distracted from a lecture, watch. So much for making friends, I think. Now they'll know that I'm the sort of person who attracts cockroaches.

Returning from job hunting, Marc finds me sitting in the front seat of my orange Hornet, staring at stars. I've stored most of my belongings in the trunk. The back seat might be big enough to serve as a bed if I tuck my knees up under my breastbone. Like a fetus, like a cannonball.

Marc knocks on the window. I roll it down.

"What are you doing?" he asks. He once worked as a cook on an offshore oil rig. He has lived in dozens of hole-in-the-wall apartments. To him, bugs are annoyances, not emergencies.

"Sitting here," I answer him.

"Are you coming inside?"

"No."

"You can't live in your car," he says.

"Why not?" I ask.

For my first graduate workshop, I turn in the story about the girl and the boy who can't get up the courage to kiss each other.

"But they obviously want to," says a classmate. "This is hard to believe. No one would take this long."

"It makes me impatient with the main character," says another. "Why doesn't she just jump his bones?"

"This is tedious," another offers. "It would be much more interesting if they just have sex."

"I have trouble believing this detail about her being really skinny even though she always eats carrot cake," says someone else.

I jot notes and pretend not to feel completely abnormal, like a girl whose first boyfriend took forever to kiss her or an unhappily married young woman or the kind of person who attracts roaches.

An exterminator arrives for his monthly rounds of the complex. He's dressed from head to foot in tan coveralls, gloves, and boots, tank belted around his waist. We chat as he aims his nozzle into cracks around the kitchen area. I am oddly in awe of him, as if he is a superhero or a priest who holds the key to exorcising my demons.

Opening the door to the closet housing a water heater that serves four apartments, he goes on talking as he squirts. Then, as if he'd just shot the starting gun for a hundred-yard dash, an army of bugs appears, bolting across the ceiling.

I leap up from my orange chair so abruptly that it pitches forward and backward in a mad rocking frenzy. The sheet of bugs starts to drop, a rainstorm of roaches pocking the floor. The rug. The table. My legs.

My legs! I scream. I dance, shaking off bugs and hallucinations of bugs.

The exterminator emerges from the closet into a chaos of screams and madly flung limbs and bugs racing and dropping and dashing every which way across the floor.

"They won't hurt you," he says, sounding puzzled.

He promises to return to fog the next week. Marc, eternally optimistic about things like this, declares that that will get rid of our roaches once and for all.

I try to believe him, that roaches will soon become a far-off memory, my thoughts freed to travel profounder avenues. In the meantime, I am writing a story about a woman whose house is infested by roaches.

I arrive home at five on Fogging Day, shaky with nervous anticipation. When I push open the apartment door, a heavy chemical smell rushes to meet me. I step into the strangely quiet room.

The floor is littered with thin brown particles, narrow fragments of harmless splinters, legs curled demurely like tangled tendrils of hair.

After inspecting my orange chair for dead bugs, I pull up my legs and rock slowly. The creaking thunders through the quiet room, the faint roars and rustles that usually make up the backdrop of my life completely absent, the apartment pervaded by the greatest silence I have ever known. The silence of no bugs.

Then I realize that the exterminator has closed the windows, blocking out sounds of traffic and lawn mowers. I plant my feet carefully on the floor. I will nudge each window open, I tell myself. Then I will plug in the vacuum and suck up the bugs.

But I will soon learn another fact about roaches. That they can hold their breaths for long periods, avoiding the worst of the poison.

My first clue is the quiver in the corner. I watch dumbfounded as a bug resurrects itself, then moves in drunken slow motion toward the drape, disappearing into its folds.

In my undergraduate poetry class, I wrote a poem in which the sun, shining through my mother's blinds, reminds her of a rippled potato chip. My mother had recently reinvented herself after being diagnosed with diabetes, walking miles a day and giving up junk food altogether, and in the poem, the potato chip becomes a symbol of my mother's survival. The repercussions of that one potato chip ripple through her life, becoming at once a symbol of desires unfulfilled but obstacles surmounted.

"But it's a potato chip," my professor said flatly. And I had to agree that a potato chip was too trivial and slim an object to carry such profound weight.

Now, when I turn in my story about the woman fighting a cockroach infestation, a story in which cockroaches become objective correlatives for all the woman's fears and unmet longings, for all the cracks in her relationships, for the shifting of her foundation, my classmates shake their heads.

"But they're *cockroaches*," they say, and I sigh, doomed to keep repeating the same mistakes.

And yet, subtly but surely, roaches notwithstanding, my life is changing. For the first time ever, I belong. My burgeoning group of friends call to chat and stop by and whisk me off to Polly's Café for vegetarian sandwiches with sprouts, or George's Majestic Lounge with the Razorback stained glass windows, or outside, to George's Beer Garden, where we go to hear Steve Pryor and the Mighty Kingsnakes on weekend nights. Mary, the manager, always says to me, "Popcorn and Diet Coke?" When the band plays, I climb the box elder and from my perch watch everyone dance. Marc is in high demand as a dance partner, since I'm too self-conscious to join in.

Marc gets a job at a local newspaper and he and I move into a new place, a townhouse in a newly remodeled Victorian house. We pack carefully and then unpack on the lawn to make sure we don't bring in any bugs. After that, we are mostly kind to each other. There are no more bugs to remind us of all the gaps and cracks and hidden places, all the unpredictable, untamed emotions that might escape when least expected. We are only mildly unhappy most of the time.

Someday, I've always hoped, the stresses of daily life will die down and my marriage turn into something stable and comfortable and reliable. Instead, it's I who am changing. Cindy teaches me to dance. Anna talks me into buying a miniskirt at the mall. Sara and I hang out at the pool on summer afternoons. Elaine and I attend aerobics class twice a week. I don't tell any of them how every three months Marc gets restless, starts saying he doesn't want to be married anymore.

But now, when Marc says that, I pause for a second. I wonder what would happen if I say that I don't want to be married either. Lately, I've developed random crushes. I have one on my friend Elaine's boyfriend, on one of the guys in my office who I argue with a lot to stave off any sexual tension, on a couple of guys down the hall. I am suddenly promiscuous in my wild attractions to men who aren't my husband, though I'm sure I would never act on them. Or would I? What if I meet someone who reminds me of Cole? What then?

I thought Marc was the cruel one, unwilling to honor his commitment to me, but what if I'm the one who decides to look for a life with someone I feel passionate about, a life without the color orange?

My heart, I fear, is transforming into a stubborn, alien, skittering creature utterly foreign to me and all the things I'm supposed to want. It's as if it's been holding its breath for years, grieving the loss of Cole. It's as if now its struggling legs are finally stirring, wobbling to their feet, testing the surrounding air.

Whenever I try to rein in my fantasies, to bring them back under control, they skitter away from me, uncooperative. My heart wants what it wants.

Often, at night, I can't sleep, too much adrenaline flowing through me, my sinuses congested, and I go outside and sit on our porch swing, tapping my feet against the floorboards and drifting back and forth until I'm a little seasick. I remember being a child on a swing, rising up into the sky, a freedom so opposite this trap I'm in, bound by these contradictory yearnings. All I can think is, I wanted my life to change, I wanted my real life to begin, but destroying my marriage and straying from all of my beliefs isn't what I meant, isn't what I wanted. Still my soft heart goes on changing, against my will, forming a shell, turning restless and reckless, shameful, untrustworthy. I lie awake every night thinking about men who aren't my husband.

Moving into this townhouse, unloading each box on the lawn, I remember shaking out the occasional roach corpse. Brown shreds, smaller than paper matchsticks, vanished into the grass, becoming one with the dirt. But then, as I reached for a saucepan, a bug staggered to its feet, sauntering along the box's cardboard flap. I stepped back. Watched, with awe, this creature, skeletal after three months with no food or water. Unable to zip in characteristic roach fashion, instead ambling unsteadily, but somehow, impossibly, still alive, rambling away to safety. I think about that as I wonder what I'm going to do about this marriage I've hung onto for so long. Is this really what I want? I wonder over and over, pacing the living room at night.

I don't know who I'm becoming. I don't know where I'm going. All I know is that my beleaguered heart beats on, insistent on survival.

FLIGHT: PART 2
Fayetteville, Arkansas

Fall 1985

MARC WAVES THE mail at me when I meet him in front of our Victorian townhouse, white with red doors, a huge wraparound porch, and a swing that bangs against the siding on windy days. The apartment's smell of new paint and carpet glue makes me happy, along with the fall's brisk air and mellowing sunlight.

Moving here, to Fayetteville, and then this apartment, have been the right decisions. Everything is so much better. Maybe the problems over the two years of our marriage really have been due to all the things we blamed them on: his health issues, the heat and humidity that drained our energy and made our house feel claustrophobic, my inability, in Pratt, to find a job that paid very

213

well, his crummy job, the roach-infested apartment we've recently fled.

Today, Marc is giddy. He's the only person in the world who has managed to get a recent photo of Walmart founder Sam Walton, notoriously camera shy, and his photograph, picked up for international syndication, appeared today in *U.S. News and World Report*. Our friends are waiting at Albert's, a dark restaurant with cracked vinyl seats. We meet here every Tuesday night for the twenty-five-cent hamburger special. My friends are bright and lively, our world electric with conversation and discovery. This is the life I've always been waiting for.

Late that night, Marc turns on the computer he bought by urging me to take out a student loan, then investing it in gold. He puts in Flight Simulator. Going to bed alone, I think about how dreams of flying are supposed to represent sex.

"Come watch me do a loop," Marc calls. "This is great."

I touch the light switches as I pass them. This apartment is so full of shocks, I easily collect and transfer them to him whenever I kiss or touch him. He, in turn, often drags his feet across the carpet as he sneaks up from behind to shock me. We both laugh at the game, but secretly I wonder if these daily exchanges of electricity, these sparks traveling between our skin, are passive-aggressive signals or last-ditch efforts at romance.

"You've got to see this," he says. I huddle on the floor of the spare bedroom, hugging my knees, looking up at the monitor.

Resting one hand on my head, he hunches over the keyboard, staring at the graphics on the screen, the instrument panel and windshield. The ground blurs beneath us as we head down the runway and tip into the air.

"We're at 10,000 feet," Marc says, his hand lifting from my hair. As we do a nose dive toward Lake Michigan, the altimeter needle spins. Marc punches keys, and the lake and sky briefly change places as the plane sweeps up into the air.

"I did it," he yells, relaxing, and the plane heads back down, aimed at the water.

The windshield cracks and everything is still.

SPLASH! the screen says.

"Aren't you coming to bed?" I ask, shivering, reaching out, then hesitating to smooth his hair that is sticking up. He's started to grow back his beard after several months of a bare chin that I never got used to; without a beard, his face seems indistinct to me. I'm not sure who he is. Now, his new growth has hit a cute scruffy stage.

"Sure, sweetie. Be there in a minute." Hands tensed over the keyboard, he's absorbed, heading down the runway again.

The blankets spark and snap as I crawl under them. Marc comes to bed after I'm asleep, and I wake long before he does. My hair crackles through the comb and each strand floats through the air. I peel socks from the inside of my sweater, which is soft and clingy, charged with electricity. I can't kiss Marc goodbye without transmitting shocks.

We don't see each other much. He works at night, goes off on freelance assignments or plays poker with his coworkers. It seems like no one ever pays him for that freelance work he's always doing. Once or twice I find a check in the mail, but mostly, everything seems to be delayed or forgotten. I'm busy grading papers and working on writing projects, and when I take breaks, I call my friends and chat for hours. I've joined a Bible study group and I scramble to make a grilled cheese sandwich before I go, but I can't find the skillet and there are only two small plates. Maybe Marc has rearranged things. The silverware drawer also seems sparser than I remember.

At lunchtime my friends and I walk down to Dickson Street for burritos and then we browse the used bookstore. At night I climb the tree at George's and watch everyone dance, and afterward, the guys from workshop say to me, "You were wild. You should have seen yourself last night." I've never developed a taste for alcohol and never actually drink. I'm amused.

"We drink and she gets drunk," my friend Elaine likes to say.

On summer days, my friend Sara and I take books to the pool or the lake and at night Marc brings home friends or invites mine over for movies and barbecues. Though the spontaneity is starting to get old and sometimes I wish he'd consult me before inviting people over, I'm ambivalent about these impromptu parties; I love the energy and friends and food and books, and I'm so much happier than I was last year. I imagine that Marc is too.

When he comes to bed after playing Flight Simulator all evening, I'm wearing a see-through nightgown that I bought a while ago but never dared to wear. Finding it in the bottom of my drawer, I've decided to try it on. "What do you think?" I ask Marc. His hand finds the ribbon that holds it together. When he yanks, it comes untied and the whole thing falls off.

"Wow," we both say, and I go to change into something cotton.

"Good night, sweetheart," he says, and drops off to sleep.

There's a storm that night. I hear him scrambling up, going to unplug his computer. I feel a rush of chilly, moist air and hear the clatter of rain on concrete before he slams the door behind him, off to take more lightning pictures.

I pretend not to be irritated that he leaves for a party on Friday night without giving me the address, telling me that he'll come to pick me up later, then never returns for me. He seems contrite afterward. He never confers with me about purchases, he never checks with me in advance about dinner gatherings and this is starting to bug me, he plans trips that don't include me and tells me about them once the plans are set. He and a friend secretly scheme to buy a house and renovate it; I only find out about it when a loan application is underway. Ultimately it's turned down, but not before another argument ensues over his refusal to consult me about important decisions. I find a letter he's written to his sister in which he doesn't mention me at all, but refers to our apartment as "my apartment" as if I don't exist.

Every time we argue, he gets more and more distant and uncommunicative. If this marriage ends, I wonder, where will I live? Will I have to find another job to pay expenses? Who will I talk to every day? What will my family and friends say? I panic when I think about this. Right now, everyone seems to regard me as mature and wise. I know that I will lose that status if I'm no longer married. I feel as if I'll be cast out of some inner circle.

One spring evening, I'm procrastinating marking the pile of student papers in front of me when Marc slams in the front door without saying hello and heads up to the computer. I trail my fingers along the light switches as I follow up behind him, waiting for static to tingle across my fingertips, but there's none. I'm at a loss as I come up behind him, flicking my finger across the back of his neck. He doesn't even notice. He squints at the screen and runs his plane into the Sears Tower. CRASH! the screen says as the windshield cracks. The program starts again, automatically; the windshield reappears, intact.

"Is something wrong?" I ask.

"No." He takes off. "Everything's fine."

"Are you sure?"

He nods as he guides the plane with one hand and reaches for my arm with the other, pulls me onto his lap, buries his head in my shoulder.

"Maybe I'm just paranoid," I say, "but it feels like something's wrong."

He releases me to save the plane from crashing. "I have to go," he says. He doesn't look at me.

"Go where?" I say. "It's 10 o'clock."

"For good," he says, his voice catching.

I toss dirty clothes, loose and limp from wear, into the washing machine. Only an hour ago, Marc told me he was leaving, staring beyond me as if he were composing a picture without me in it. I couldn't even protest through the shock that felt like calm inevitability. His blue socks with the green Bioguard thread are still shaped like his feet, with little knobs where his ankles filled them out. I watch the machine fill, the clothes swish and churn. I fold his underwear the way he likes it, but even when I put away the clean clothes, his dresser drawers seem emptier than usual.

Often, during the day, I can picture what he's doing: angling modeling lights, setting up backdrops, driving to shoot a grass fire for a newspaper or a new car model for an ad agency. But this time, I have no idea where he is. My skin aches with a kind of finality. I go to bed because I can't think of anything else to do, and I lie, skin fevered, bones heavy, nowhere near sleep. I think about the "Can This Marriage Be Saved?" column in the *Ladies' Home Journals* my mother subscribes to. When something goes wrong in a marriage, even if the husband is drinking or having affairs, the woman is told that she has to take responsibility for what she has done to drive him away. I try to figure out what I've done.

At 4:00 a.m., at the sound of a key in the lock, I lie still, afraid to breathe.

In the living room, I find Marc unloading all the missing things from a new 30-gallon plastic trash can: clothes, plates, books, measuring cups and a can opener, a pillow.

A pillow? How did I not miss a whole pillow?

"I can't do it," Marc says, surfacing from the trash can with a handful of silverware, a razor and comb, a checkbook. He tosses it to me. Inside, in an account bearing only his name, he has entered pages of freelance checks, three thousand dollars' worth.

"A few days ago, I rented an apartment," he says. "I've been planning this for months, buying things, collecting things, having all my freelance checks mailed to me at work so that I could leave. Disappear. Not have to face you."

I push the checkbook away from me on the kitchen table while Marc puts away silverware, plates, the can opener. He slams cabinets and drawers and opens a beer.

"Why?" I ask.

"I'm just a lousy husband. I'm no good at being married. It makes me feel confined."

"Why?" is all I seem to be able to say. I feel as if I've backed away and am watching a play or a movie, as if I know all the dialogue and gestures before they happen, the way he leaves his beer to pace the room, the way I crush a Kleenex in my palm, gritting back tears.

"I didn't really want to leave," he says.

"Then why did you?"

"I was starting to panic, I guess. I feel so cooped up."

"Are you having an affair?"

"Are you kidding?" He scoops up his beer, his tone convincingly incredulous. "That would be more of what I don't want. I just want to be alone sometimes. I don't want the responsibility of another person."

Outside, darkness is turning pink. Cars pass occasionally. Squares of light checker the rows of windows at the apartment complex across the street.

"Why did we get married?" I ask.

"I was afraid of the future," he finally answers. "Why did you marry me?"

"I thought you wanted me," I say. "I thought someone in the world ought to get what they wanted."

"I did," he says. "I do." He swipes the checkbook and sticks it in his pocket. "I'm closing this account today. Please don't give up on me."

I feel weirdly calm for the first time, considering the possibility that our marriage will end. A suspicion is taking root: there might be worse things. As Marc empties the trash can and folds and hangs his clothes and replaces books on shelves and socks and underwear in drawers, I banish this thought. I'm not ready for it yet. I resolve to change. I will make our marriage work. I won't mind when he's distant, won't argue when he stays out late without calling me or when he fails to consult me about decisions.

But still. I think about how in Flight Simulator, every time the plane crashes, it magically repairs itself. Does Marc really think we can push reset and swoop off into some new, clean beginning?

"Let's just go to sleep," Marc says. He carries a new toothbrush and razor, still in their packages, to the bathroom. He tosses the pillow back onto the bed.

Before he lies down, before he drops off to sleep, he kisses me, the tiny ache of a shock passing between us.

Can This Marriage Be Saved? A Quiz

9. Why would your husband say that he married you?

a. Because, he said the first week, he liked being in love.

b. Because, he said the first week, he wanted to wake up to you every day.

c. Because, he said five years later, he was afraid of the future.

THINGS OF ETERNAL WORTH

ONE MONDAY NIGHT that first fall in Fayetteville, I leave behind our townhouse and its lingering smells of new paint and carpet glue and steer through the brisk air and wood smoke drifting down from Mount Sequoyah. I drive past the cemetery where, on top of a grave marked with the name HUDSON, someone has centered a huge rock. Rock Hudson just died of AIDS. I already feel sad for the day I'll be leaving our apartment and this town for good.

I drive on, away from Marc and our troubled marriage and my irreverent new friends who like to gather at bars and burger joints and sing along with the jukebox, pretending salt shakers are microphones. I feel like I'm leading a secret double life as I stop at Subway for a sandwich, then head to Springdale.

I didn't tell anyone where I was going and now I'm not sure why I'm here, in a sanctuary of shiny walnut pews with burgundy cushions where gentle dabs of perfume on earlobes and wrists accumulate into an overpowering sneeze-inducing reek. I'm instantly congested again, unable to breathe. Bare-legged in an indigenous woven cotton jumper from Guatemala and ballet flats, I'm surrounded by stay-at-home moms in jeans and frazzled hair and businesswomen in shoulder pads and hose and low-heeled pumps that match their fitted suits.

From the pulpit, the leader welcomes us. Each week, she tells us, we'll receive printed questions and scriptures, and we should write our answers before each meeting.

I can do this, I think. I'm a creative writing student. I like to write.

"I don't know about this tone of forlorn ennui," my professor recently scrawled on one of my stories. Maybe he's right, maybe I'm too serious. I worry too much. My new friends joke that I should get a personalized license plate that says, "4LRN-N-WE."

"Why are we here?" the Bible study leader asks us. "Why should we take time out of our busy schedules, away from husbands and children . . ."

I stop listening. Why am I here? Because I'm so full of turmoil all the time. Because my marriage has been in crisis every day since the wedding, because sometimes I still think about Cole and wish not for him exactly, but for someone who makes me feel the way he did. Because I feel my life heading away from the path I always imagined for myself. I'm here because I'm afraid of losing the reverent childhood self that was sure of her salvation, afraid of embracing the things of this world I was always warned about in Sunday school, things like secular humanism and transcendental meditation. Because I'm having trouble giving up a vision of my life instilled in me in my youth, a vision in which I am a wife worth more than rubies whose progeny will rise up to call me blessed.

Instead, I'm married to a man who makes me laugh and charms my friends but has no interest in spending time with me. He goes to bars and parties and poker nights, forgetting all about me, returning home at all hours half-drunk and saturated with cigarette smoke. He threatens to end our marriage if I complain. I know I'll be the first divorcée in the history of my family. The question is not if, but when. I live with a sense of persistent dread.

When I look back years later, I will answer the question of why I was there differently. I will see that it wasn't so much about reverence or salvation as it was clinging to an old self I was afraid to let go of, one who had been raised to construct her life around faith, because I wasn't sure who I'd be without it. I will someday understand that, in fact, Bible study gave me a framework for figuring out what I believed and what I didn't, for reviewing my life and putting it in context. That process would save me, but not in the way I originally expected.

After another hymn, we disperse to Sunday school classrooms to meet our assigned groups. Mine is the Under Thirties, led by a stay-at-home mom named Lisa who says that sometimes all she wants to do is stare out the window with a cup of tea. I like her for admitting this, feel drawn to her wistfulness.

All of the women glow when they mention their husbands. The only unmarried ones are best friends with cropped hair. Anywhere else, I'd assume they were lesbian partners.

The one named Susan who walks with a swagger and has a husky voice tells us she's going to be a doctor, but first she and Claire are signing on to go to Africa as missionaries. Everyone looks awed and from then on defers to Susan as The Smart One in the group. Claire will heretofore be referred to as "Susan's Friend."

I introduce myself awkwardly: twenty-two, married for two years, a teaching assistant in the Arkansas MFA program, a transplant from Kansas. I try to fake the glow of Christian married happiness. I don't mention that I don't go to church, or that my husband is not a believer, or that I have my own doubts. I suspect that even without saying those things, I'm already staking out my territory as The Weird One in the group.

Weeks 1–2: Teachings on Creation

In the Beginning was the Word, and the Word was with God, and the Word was God. —John 1:1

What does this suggest about the first book of Genesis?

I find myself daydreaming over my lesson, thinking about how God spoke words and whole worlds appeared. Let there be light, He said, and there was light. I can still remember a moment when I was three or four, sitting in the back seat of a powder blue Impala, the shapes on my department store candy counter bag forming themselves into a word: *Sears*.

In that moment, whole worlds broke open, leaping from a background blur of blinking store names, lit marquees, small green street signs. They turned into meaning, magically, obediently, like when my weight on the sidewalk flung open Sears' automatic doors. And all of a sudden, the world held a new kind of excitement, made a new kind of sense. Some of my friends say their real lives began when they met their boyfriends or got married. Mine, I think, began the day I learned to read.

Sometimes, I long again for a life that felt complete just because it had words and stories in it.

"So what about this?" says Lisa. "I don't know if I understand this verse."

Claire looks expectantly at Susan, and everyone else follows. "*The word* actually refers to Christ," Susan says. "He was the source of scripture, who existed from the beginning."

Everyone nods thoughtfully as if this makes total sense to them. I blush because my answer is apparently so much more personal and less pious than anyone else's, and I feel a very unchristian jealousy that Susan has secured her position as The Smart One.

> God said, "Let the water under the sky be gathered in one place, and let dry ground appear." And it was so.
> —Genesis 1:9
> According to the Bible, how long did it take God to accomplish this task?

At twelve or thirteen, I learned in school about continental drift. I was excited: If a day in the Bible was a metaphor for billions of years, weren't the Bible and science compatible? God had spoken into being one big body of water and one big continent, and then, over time, the land had divided into several masses, edges like puzzle pieces that had once all been locked together.

Back when I had this revelation that I didn't have to choose between science and the Bible, I was still so certain of who I was. I saw myself as all of a piece, my life stretching out ahead of me like an uninterrupted picture, before the jigsaw cuts and jagged edges of experience that created spaces and gaps, crevices and fissures, breaches and rifts.

"Some people think a day in the Bible really means billions of years," says Claire with a sidelong glance at Susan, who is, after all, pre-med, but she just nods encouragingly. "But the Bible clearly says it was a day. Twenty-four hours."

"I think it insults God to imagine that He would need more time than that," a woman named Julie says.

Everyone concurs: The world was created, exactly as it is today, in six days.

Everyone except me. I keep quiet.

Week 5: God's View of Marriage

God created man in His own image, in the image of
God He created him; male and female He created them.
—Genesis 1:27
Whosoever shall put away his wife, and marry another,
committeth adultery against her. And if a woman shall
put away her husband, and be married to another, she
committeth adultery. —Mark 10:11–12
What do these verses suggest about God's sacred purpose
for marriage?

Marc never asks me about Bible study. He works long hours at the local newspaper and then goes to poker night, or he shows up at home with all of his coworkers, having impulsively invited them over for dinner. He thinks I'm rude if I don't welcome them wholeheartedly on the spur of the moment. Everyone thinks of him as easygoing and spontaneous, and I'm pretty sure they consider me to be uptight because I want advance warning, because I feel awkward if near-strangers show up when I'm wearing an old T-shirt, eating a Pop-Tart, or doing sit-ups while I watch *Jeopardy!* Marc thinks I'm defective because I like privacy and solitude. I wish he weren't quite so oblivious to other people's emotional landscapes.

"My husband," the women at Bible study like to say, infusing the words with pride:

"My husband goes to church every week, but he's not a believer. I'm praying that the Lord will convict him," says one.

"My husband hates it when I sew at night. He wants me to watch TV with him," says another.

A wave of yearning crashes over me, to do ordinary things, go to church together, watch TV together at night, have quiet, intimate evenings rather than a houseful of people all the time.

"I used to love to read," says Lisa. "But my husband and I agreed that I wasn't paying enough attention to my other duties, so I had to quit."

Yanked abruptly out of my desire for the mundane routines the others take for granted, I stare at Lisa in horror and realize that, hard as I've tried to keep my marriage going, there are limits to my devotion.

Week 8: On How God Punishes Sinners
And they said, Go to, let us build us a city and a tower, whose top may reach unto heaven; and let us make us a name, lest we be scattered abroad upon the face of the whole earth.... And the Lord said, ... let us go down, and there confound their language, that they may not understand one another's speech. —Genesis 11:1–7

While he was still speaking, another came and said, "The
fire of God fell from heaven and burned up the sheep
and the servants and consumed them, and I alone have
escaped to tell you." —Job 1:16
What do these passages suggest about God's punishment
to sinners?

I don't know how to answer this. It's always puzzled me
that the whole Babel thing is such a threat. I remember
wondering as a child how come none of this stuff happens
anymore—people abruptly scattered across the earth,
lightning striking them dead? Why don't seas part, whales
swallow people who live to tell about it, people rise from
the dead? Why aren't these events reported in the news?
But maybe it's a good thing that this stuff doesn't happen
anymore. It seems to me that people would be better off
communicating with each other, and I don't understand
God's deliberate efforts to prevent that.

"Sometimes God sends disasters to remind us to mend
our ways," Julie says.

I steel myself for someone to mention the AIDS epidem-
ic, for Claire and Susan to say something about their mission to save Africans. But thankfully, the moment passes.

"We don't really see good miracles much nowadays,
either," says a woman named Kelly whose husband is also
named Kelly. "I mean, no one walks on water or changes
water into wine anymore. I think that God doesn't really
need to send signs anymore to prove that He exists."

"Right," Lisa says. "Christianity has been around for
almost two thousand years."

Week 15 is our Christmas party. We meet at Julie's house
for coffee and cookies and fellowship. Julie is not much

older than me, but she lives in an actual house, not an apartment. The porch is outlined by Christmas lights, no bulbs burnt out, and there are two newish cars parked side by side in the driveway. Inside, a couch and coffee table are like stranded islands in the empty room, a TV hidden inside a cabinet in the corner, no heap of camera equipment, messes of magazines, piles of papers, shelves of books. No books at all. This bothers me.

Week 28: God's Commands Regarding Witnessing and Worship

At the mouth of two witnesses, or three witnesses, shall he that is worthy of death be put to death; but at the mouth of one witness he shall not be put to death. —Deuteronomy 17:6

For where two or three are gathered together in my name, there am I in the midst of them. —Matthew 18:20

What do these verses tell us about God's commands regarding witnessing and worship?

I recall a youth minister who maintained that, to get an audience with God, two or more of us must gather in His name. It was the first I'd ever heard that my previous prayers didn't count because I'd prayed them alone. The youth minister also said that you weren't a real Christian unless you spread the word to other people, and that your prayers didn't count unless you ended them by saying, "In Jesus's name I pray." This was the first time I understood that Christianity was a club that I might not qualify to join, a club for outgoing people, not shy ones like me.

The other youth group girls, cheeks bright with blush, eyes shadowed by blue makeup, bracelets and earrings jangling, talked enthusiastically about witnessing to others, something that sounded excruciating to me. Then, after the lesson was over, they switched back to discussing boys and shopping and other girls, and it awed me that they could consider themselves Christians and still be so preoccupied with the things of this world. Then abruptly they shifted back to reverence, singing,

They'll know we are Christians by our love, by our love
Yes they'll know we are Christians by our love.

I was confused by all of these rapid shifts. I wasn't actually sure that I would automatically know these girls were Christians by their love. I felt like a weirdo around them. Certainly not particularly loved. Or, to be honest, loving.

And now I wonder if the women in my Bible study group are grown-up versions of my Sunday school classmates. Though we are all more mature and I am less judgmental, I find their lives with husbands and without books to be mysterious. I feel little spark of connection. It's becoming more obvious to me that no matter how hard I try, I will never belong to their world any more than I belonged to the world of the youth group girls.

I know these women have their struggles. Julie has been unable to conceive. Lisa fights to make ends meet with her husband's paycheck. Quiet, delicate Claire chafes at times, just a little, at the opinions of confident, brash Susan. I remind myself that there is more to these women than meets the eye.

Today, they unite in laughing at the discussion question, since we aren't planning to put anyone to death. They all have their struggles, but they agree with each other about the power of witnessing to others.

And just as when I was a teenager, I find the idea excruciating.

Year Two, Week 1: On Finding Comfort during Difficult Times

The Lord is my shepherd; I shall not want.
He maketh me to lie down in green pastures: he leadeth me beside the still waters.
He restoreth my soul: he leadeth me in the paths of righteousness for his name's sake. —Psalm 23
How do you find comfort in God's word?

I don't finish my lesson. When we go around the room and update the group about our summer vacations, I don't mention how tense and distracted Marc has been when he's not angry and remote. I don't mention the party he went to on Friday night without giving me the address or coming back to get me as he promised. I don't mention how when we argued, he got so angry that he put his fist through a wall.

The other women talk about all the reasons they lean on these verses. But not because their husbands might leave them.

I've always found solace in these verses too. I remember memorizing the Twenty-third Psalm as a teenager. But now I'm too restless, too anguished, to feel soothed as the life I imagined for myself drifts slowly away.

Week 5: Preparing for the End Times

And many of those who sleep in the dust of the ground will awake, these to everlasting life, but the others to disgrace and everlasting contempt. —Daniel 12:2

There will be a great tribulation, such as has not
occurred since the beginning of the world until now, nor
ever shall. —Matthew 24:21
Are you ready for the end times and Christ's return?

The end times. All I can think of is the inevitable end
of my marriage as I sit at the kitchen table, trying to
concentrate on my Bible study questions while stray cats
yowl below me, gathering under the house, snarling and
growling and thumping as they fight or mate. Periodically,
the landlord gathers all of the stray cats and takes them
to the SPCA. Outside the kitchen window, the porch
swing that Marc took down so it wouldn't bang against
the side of the house in a windstorm has skidded over to
the railing.

I try to shift my focus to the Second Coming. Years
ago, my mother made our whole family watch a TV movie
about it. In the movie, a farmer in a wheat field turned to
speak to his partner and found the tractor seat empty. A
woman washed dishes, prattling on, not noticing that her
husband was gone, newspaper askew on the table, steam
rising from his coffee.

One will be taken, one will be left, people kept saying.
He will come like a thief in the night.

It terrified me that I secretly hoped to be left behind.
That I secretly yearned to just stay on earth and finish
junior high and have a boyfriend. And now, I still want to
be left behind. I want a chance to straighten out the mess
that is my life, somehow, though I don't have any idea how.

"I hope I'll be the one taken," Claire says fervently, and
with her bigger hand, Susan envelopes Claire's tiny one.
Something intense seems to pass between them.

"I have to work harder on that," Susan says with a sigh, and I like her better, but don't admit to my own yearning for the things of this world. Love, writing, books, children someday.

I smile at the group and think, *take them, not me.*

Week 12: On Being Part of a Community
And let us consider how to stir up one another to love and good works ... encouraging one another. —Hebrews 10:24–25
We, being many, are one body in Christ, and every one members one of another. —Romans 12:4–5
What do these verses tell us about the role of church members?

I remember my first date with Cole, accompanying him to his church. By comparison to St. Stephan's carved walnut pews, thick carpet, padded kneelers, and more mournful doxology, my pine-pewed church seemed tacky and stark. Episcopalians used the word *trespasses* in the Lord's Prayer, clearly a more upscale and refined word than *debts*, which felt gauche, as if we were publicly discussing finances with the Lord. Although I found Episcopal hymns so unpredictable that I had trouble singing them and so high-pitched that even the sopranos screeched, the music seemed more stately and majestic, less folksy. Cole lit up when I told him that I could imagine converting.

I thought that my parents would be thrilled by my plan to marry a priest, but my mom sounded disapproving when she said, "If you marry a clergyman, you'll have to entertain a lot." What I heard was: *Are you deluded? You hide in your room all the time and have no social skills.*

"There's a lot of alcoholism in churches that serve wine," my dad said.

I was dashed. I'd been imagining an admirably virtuous future while my parents instead envisioned me with an alcoholic husband and a parsonage full of needy strangers. It was beginning to seem like church people would disapprove of me no matter what I did, would keep trying to convert me to what I was already converted to, would keep trying to convince me to join a club I thought I'd already joined.

Back when Cole dumped me, then remained distant for months before he abruptly left town without leaving a forwarding address, I was sure there must be something wrong with me that had driven him away. The same thing that had drawn unwanted attention from boys in the eighth grade. Was it the same mysterious thing that caused other Christians to disapprove of me, to refuse to fully accept me as one of them?

Maybe things are different here: Susan praises me because I showed her how to format her thesis, and Julie and I laugh a lot, and when Lisa moves away, we're all sad. I like the humor and spunk of our new leader, Chris, who makes lots of jokes about her fiancé and her upcoming wedding. But I will never have the kinds of conversations with these women that I do with my grad school friends, passionate and intense and truthful, truthful except for those parts of my life I can never reveal.

Week 22: On Not Yoking Ourselves to Unbelievers
Be ye not unequally yoked together with unbelievers: for what fellowship hath righteousness with unrighteousness? and what communion hath light with darkness?
—2 Corinthians 6:14

What does this tell us about making alliances (including marriages) with unbelievers?

Numb, grieving the loss of Cole years ago, I see now how I took the path of least resistance when I succumbed to the pressure to become engaged to Marc. I felt guilty about being involved with a lapsed Catholic, but he pursued me so intently, I also felt unable to stop the momentum.

At Single Direction, a Presbyterian group I attended with my friend Ty during college, after Marc and I had become engaged, we were always hearing warnings about uniting ourselves with sinfulness. I felt permanently conflicted, feeling like I would never fit in with these people, knowing that according to the lesson, Marc was all wrong for me. Yet I was way more comfortable around him than I was around fellow believers. So where did I fit, anyway?

One night, I ducked out of Single Direction and followed strains of organ music to a dark chapel. Up front in a pool of lamplight, an organist fingered chords.

Ty found me there. She'd been talking to the minister about me, she said, her voice too loud in the empty dark chapel after the organist gathered her music, clicked off the lamp, and left. "He asked if you were a Christian, and I said I didn't know."

"You don't know?" I repeated.

"I told him that you never talk about it, and he said that's the same thing as not being one at all," she said. "I told him you were still a spiritual baby, but you have lots of potential."

I stared at the diamond on my finger, dull there in the dark as raindrops blotched the stained glass. In the light it twinkled like a little star, so alive with color that the diamond itself seemed to disappear. This diamond had ushered me into a club, into a sense of belonging: suddenly, other engaged couples at Single Direction and married women at the student newspaper treated me like I was one of them. But I wondered: Was I sacrificing my inner light for something false and material? If I had to make a choice, which would I choose? My faith? My upcoming marriage? Neither?

It scared me to think that I might choose neither.

Chris, our new leader, tells us that she has to resign. Her fiancé has been married before. The Bible study organization prohibits anyone who is divorced or married to a divorcée from being a leader.

Chris is cheerfully philosophical at the idea that the organization is essentially accusing her of committing adultery, but her demotion catches me off guard. I feel stricken by this evidence of what I've always suspected: that leaving my marriage would mean also giving up on ever fully belonging to a church community. It would mean being an outsider from everything my upbringing taught me was important. I don't understand how Chris can be okay with being treated like a pariah just because the man she will be marrying is divorced. How is that her fault? What kind of organization is this, to be so intent on preventing anyone whose marriage didn't work out from ever finding love again?

<u>Week 32: On Supporting Missionaries and Mission Work</u>
And in very deed for this cause have I raised thee up,
for to shew in thee my power; and that my name may be
declared throughout all the earth. —Exodus 9:16
What should our attitude be toward missionaries and
mission work?

Our last meeting of the year is held at Kelly and her husband Kelly's bookless house and doubles as a goodbye party for Susan and Claire. They'll leave for Africa in June.

Sue and Claire regale us with stories about the batteries of tests they have undergone during their training, including the MMPI, to be sure they're mentally sound.

Sue's favorite question was, "I sometimes feel that I don't really exist." I gather from her derision that the obvious correct mentally sound missionary-worthy answer is *False*.

"I remember when I was a kid, wondering if I existed," I say.

Most of my group smiles tolerantly. I've gotten braver over the years, admitting that I admire Paul not for his religious fervor but because he managed to write in prison, pointing out metaphors just because I like them, not because they illuminate my relationship with God. I often catch myself smiling at things that the others take seriously, like a news story about the Arkansas community that tried to ban a book called *Making It with Mademoiselle* before they discovered it contained sewing patterns from a women's magazine.

"No, really," I say now. "I used to wonder if maybe existence was this huge cosmic joke being played on me."

Smiles falter and Susan snorts, and I realize that I've just revealed my own mental unsoundness for missionary work.

Year 3, Week 1: On Embracing the Truth of Christ's Freedom

And you will know the truth, and the truth will make you free. —John 8:32

What does it mean to know the truth of God's word?
What is the difference between being set free and being
made free by truth?

It's fall again. Only a few months ago, Marc hid freelance checks in a secret account and spirited away household items. He planned to disappear so he didn't have to face me. To disappear like Cole did. I lie awake at night because my sinuses are congested and I can't breathe, wondering, what about me makes men disappear?

I'd vowed to be a better wife, more patient and forbearing when Marc didn't have time for me. And he'd vowed, for the first time, to try to be a better husband, and he had been. He was more considerate, more clearly committed to me than I've ever seen him, and yet I was less and less sure why I've fought so hard to save this marriage, more and more guilty about how detached I feel.

A tall guy with a deep voice and a glib manner that seems like a front for secret depth pauses in my office doorway to introduce himself. He's new to the program. We talk in the hallway and mailroom and doorways, and for a few days I neglect to mention that I'm married. "He gets all starry-eyed when he sees you," a classmate tells me. "He looks moonstruck."

Jon writes stories about guys who have crushes on tall blondish women with glasses. "Have you given up on love altogether, Nancy?" he asks me. Or another time, with a penetrating look: "I know about your marriage." As if he sees right through it, through me, sees me fully.

I lie awake that night, daydreamy and distracted and guilty. I can't stop thinking about Jon. After years of apologizing to Marc, making promises, insisting that things will get better, now that Marc seems to be putting forth some effort, all I can think about is another man. "So Anxious You Want to Scream?" blares the headline on the cover of one of the women's magazines in the pile on my bedside table. My mother always passes them on to me when she's done with them.

I pace, I fret, I stop eating, I trace again and again the moment that Jon stopped in my office doorway and asked me if I could tape together a rip in his shirt. The moment that we both watched as I smoothed out the tape, feeling his arm underneath. How, as if mesmerized, he reached out and petted my hair as if I was a cat.

I relive that gesture over and over instead of training my distracted focus on my Bible study lesson. I stay up late at night paging through my mother's discarded magazines, *Good Housekeeping, McCall's, Woman's Day, Ladies' Home Journal*. The articles are all geared toward economically comfortable women with stable marriages, children, careers that take a back seat to everything else. The articles are all about sex and solving conflicts and juggling schedules. I take quizzes to figure out my exercise and relationship and negotiation styles and what hair color suits me best and how to find the perfect skin care routine. I read the "Can This Marriage Be Saved?" column in *Ladies' Home Journal*, the background, her take on things, his take on things, the counselor's advice. Usually, the counselor thinks that the marriage can be saved, if only the woman takes responsibility for the problems.

I start to feel so inadequate about the discrepancy between the life depicted in these magazines and my reality, I finally ask my mother not to give them to me anymore. I tell her that the glossy pages give me eyestrain. It may really be the lack of sleep that gives me eyestrain.

I write a story about a woman whose husband tries to leave her, and my professor says to me, "How old are you?"

"Almost twenty-five," I say.

"In the next five years, you are going to discover that for every effect there is a cause," he growls at me.

I don't know what this means exactly. That there are reasons that I don't understand why Cole disappeared, why Marc tried to leave? Is it possible that Cole's disappearance wasn't some odd, random event, but maybe had a cause? For the first time in all of these years, newly confident because of Jon's attention and my group of friends and my understanding that there are things I'm good at, I am, I think, ready to hear the truth.

Tracking down Cole isn't so hard. I call his brother in Chicago. "Oh, are you one of his friends from Kansas City?" his brother asks. A kitten leaps into my lap, one of a pair of kittens Marc brought home a few weeks ago. It kneads its claws against my jeans. I gently push it away.

"From Kansas," I say, and wonder later if he'd have given me Cole's number if I'd said I was a childhood friend from Wichita. If Cole maybe didn't really want to hear from people from a painful part of his life from which he'd struggled to break free.

"He's in New York City," his brother says. "He manages a bookstore. Hang on." And then, just like that, he returns and gives me Cole's phone number.

Outside, it's dark, the early dark of November, a sign that winter is coming. Marc is covering a City Council meeting in Springdale and won't be home for a couple of hours. The kittens chase each other across the floor. The TV that Marc had bought with all of the freelance checks he'd been stockpiling looms before me. The TV and the kittens were his affirmation of his new commitment to our marriage: he was spending money on something that both of us would enjoy and bringing home pets that would give us a common purpose.

Before I can think about it long enough to get nervous, I dial.

Cole answers on the second ring.

"Cole?" I say. "This is Nancy."

"Oh." He sounds taken aback. The warmth leaches from his voice, replaced by stiff politeness, as he says, "Wow." I grip the phone so tight my hand aches.

"It's been a long time," I say. "So how are you?" It feels like the walls are closing in around me so that there is only me, this couch, this phone, Cole's voice, a kitten snuggling against my leg, purring.

We struggle through an awkward conversation. He tells me about his job at a Waldenbooks in Staten Island and I update him about my year in Pratt and two years in Arkansas. I ask about his brothers and sister. He asks about my family. We're very polite.

I finally say, "You just kind of disappeared."

"I know, I lost touch with everyone," he answers, sounding regretful but offering no explanation. "I should keep in better touch."

I can hear the neighbors' voices through the wall. Headlights from a car flood my front window. Kittens sleep. The world goes on around me, but nothing makes sense. I may never get this. May never understand why Cole disappeared so abruptly.

But I don't know how to ask, so instead I write down his address and give him mine. "Let's keep in touch," I say, but I don't believe that we really will.

"Okay, well, thanks for calling," he says. In a couple of seconds, we're going to say our goodbyes and hang up and

I'll never know. I need to know. And so I say, with awkward suddenness, "Any women?"

I will cringe later at my choice of words. Not "Do you have a girlfriend" or "Are you married," but "Any women?" Like something in me knows, has always known the truth, even if I've never admitted it to myself.

"What?" his voice comes back loud and clear, as if the mouthpiece had been slipping and now he has hitched it up again.

"Any women?" I repeat, and now my face is burning with embarrassment, wishing I'd found a better way to ask about his love life.

There's a long silence, or so it seems. And then he takes a deep breath. "Nancy," he says. "I'm gay."

"Oh, I always wondered," I manage to reply somehow without missing a beat, because in an instant it is all so obvious, though I don't remember ever wondering, though I'm surprised at how unsurprised I am. How is it possible that I have never consciously wondered this? How is it possible to completely shut out such a possibility for so many years? How can the human mind conceal such obvious truths from itself, suppress so completely what it doesn't want to absorb? I vaguely recall the note Cole gave me after we broke up, telling me he sometimes doubted his sexuality. I was too naïve or too in denial to understand it, which at this moment seems impossibly ludicrous.

Suddenly, Cole starts to talk, his voice so much more relaxed that I realize just how tight it was throughout the earlier part of our conversation, as tight as my fist that clutched the phone and now loosens, still aching. "I met my partner, Jack, in Kansas City, and we moved here together," he says. "We've been together a few years."

"I remember that you wanted to be a priest," I say. Sweat is no longer gluing my palm to the phone receiver. I have never felt so relieved, so transformed: in a split second, in two words from Cole, it was like my life suddenly made sense. Like the land masses have locked back together, the ocean once again all one body, the earth all one continent, just as God had spoken it into being, the whole world so busy reconfiguring itself around me that I can barely muster the energy to finish this conversation.

"Yeah, I guess that was a sign. I really didn't want to be gay." He sounds apologetic. "I haven't totally given up my religious beliefs. I still go to church some. The Episcopal church is relatively accepting of gays."

"That's good," I say, or something equally inane, and we wind down again, making promises to keep in touch that sound more sincere than our earlier ones.

After we hang up, I sit completely still for an hour as if all of my spaces and gaps, crevices and fissures, breaches and rifts, are vanishing, briefly turning my life into one smooth surface. All the things I've always thought were my fault maybe weren't my fault at all.

I remember being a little girl on a swing, wondering if I really existed. Was that the flip side of believing that the world revolved around me? For many years I've imagined that everything had something to do with me, Cole's anguish, his disappearance, Marc's restlessness. So maybe it doesn't. Maybe none of it has really been about me at all.

A dawning sense of freedom gradually stirs me from my reverie. I want to tell someone about this right now. But I don't call any of my friends.

Instead, I wait for Marc to come home.

When the front door slams, I rise to greet him. "You won't believe what happened," I say as he shrugs off his canvas briefcase and kicks off his shoes. "I talked to Cole. I found him in New York."

Marc scoops up a kitten and sits down as my words tumble over each other. I explain, somewhat incoherently, how, in an instant, I've been absolved of all the blame that has haunted me for years, the suspicion that there's something wrong with me. Cole is gay. That's all. It wasn't me at all. Even though I didn't consciously know this until tonight, it's like my subconscious has been sorting through it for years, preparing itself to accept completely that Cole is who he is and it has nothing to do with me.

Marc is happy that I'm happy, even if he doesn't fully understand. He asks questions and listens to the answers, and I feel a pang that this happiness is one more step in a direction that will lead to the end of our marriage.

That night, I lie awake for a long time, thinking about how the story I've always believed about my life, the story that led me to marry young and live with unhappiness, isn't, after all, the right story. How the story of who I was and what my future looked like can be revised, reinterpreted, endlessly reconfigured, just like any other story.

Week 4: On Living a Life of Virtue
Who can find a virtuous woman? for her price is far above rubies.... Her children arise up, and call her blessed; her husband also, and he praiseth her. —Proverbs 31:10–28
What does it mean to be virtuous? How much time do you waste in conversations without substance? Is your speech enlightening, helpful, and instructive? Do you fill your time with activities that have eternal worth?

"Don't you worry that you turn men gay?" Jon teases me, but I just laugh, because it has never occurred to me to interpret the story that way. "But a few months ago, you told me that everything with Cole would make sense if he were gay," my friend Sara says, but I don't remember saying that. Or at least, I don't remember really thinking about my offhand comment.

Later, the kittens skitter and tumble across the living room carpet while I slip on a cardigan and settle down to do my Bible study lesson. There's a quiche in the oven and outside, someone is raking leaves. Soon, I'm afraid, I'm going to lose cozy peaceful evenings like this, I'm going to have to completely reconfigure my whole life and habits and routine.

The Bible study lesson is about activities and speech of eternal worth. It's about our duty to sacrifice pleasure, comfort, wealth, and status so as not to "stumble" others. I run my fingers over the back of the green couch, curved like a seashell, that Marc and I bought together. When we moved into this duplex with its small rooms and steep staircase leading to bedrooms with sloping attic ceilings, I'd hoped for a new beginning. I'd willed the stresses in our marriage to die down; I'd resolved to make things work. I had refused to consider that my marriage, like the Bible study, were stepping-stones to the solution, not themselves the solutions after all.

I think about how for every effect there is a cause. I read the same sentence over and over: "Have you abolished pointless conversation, trivial gossip, silly magazines, and insipid TV shows from your daily life?" the notes ask. "Do you fill your time with activities that have eternal worth?"

The sun shines through a prism in the window, scattering rainbows that the kittens chase, pouncing on them in the shifting light. I yearn for a settled life of pointless conversations, of long, aimless chats with my friends and with Jon. I yearn for occasional trashy novels and insipid TV shows. Somewhere along the way, my longing to spend evenings in mundane activities with Marc, cooking or watching TV together, has vanished.

I reread the Proverbs verses in my King James Bible and my New International Version. This worthwhile wife, worth more than rubies, rejoices in the days to come in the King James but laughs at the days to come in the NIV. Why? Such laughter strikes me as ruthless and smug, not joyful. When did I last laugh joyfully?

Suddenly, I'm paging madly through my Bible, checking the concordance, finding only thirteen biblical references to laughter: Jesus laughs scoffingly at the wicked. In the Beatitudes, all who laugh "will mourn and weep." Abraham and Sarah laugh skeptically at being promised a child because they're so old. At least Isaac's name means "he laughs," but mostly biblical laughter doesn't signal happiness or even bravado. It lacks mirth, expressing judgment or doubt. True happy laughter is shallow, a distraction from the Lord.

Last night, Jon and I sat outside, huddled in jackets, at George's Beer Garden. The sinking sun's diffuse light transformed rust- and mustard-colored leaves to bronze and gold, gray trunks to silver. We shivered and ate free happy hour popcorn and laughed and Jon told me that he considered himself a humanist. A secular humanist, I joked, remembering being warned away from those as a child. We laughed, the sort of laughter I'd thought of as frivolous during my earnestly pious childhood. We talked about books, language, words.

Now I rise from the table, take the quiche out of the oven, feed the kittens. Then I pack up my Bible study lesson, leaving it unfinished, thinking how in the beginning was the word, words that were words, not just metaphors for something else. Words and stories feel incompatible with my fundamentalist upbringing: How can I believe in the unwaveringly literal in the face of the inexactness of language and the faultiness of memory? I'm attracted to a man who isn't my husband, though I understand that once I embrace ambivalence and ambiguity, once I give up all certainty, that's when I will fully cross the line. But already I have reached a milestone. I can't go back to Bible study.

Late into the night, Marc still not home, my future still unconfronted, I go on agonizing in our low-ceilinged bedroom. Outside, trees brush against each other in the wind, and from far away, a dog barks. Leaves blow along the ground, shuffling against each other like glass crackling. But for me, time feels suspended as I think about Jon. I'm worn out from emotional turmoil, from questioning everything I have ever believed. All I want is to shut off my brain for just a while, to relax and shut out this turbulence.

Purring kittens curl up next to me as I daydream about Jon, page through silly magazines, and watch the leaves out the window shiver in a breeze. Such moments of intermittent peace feel so worthy, I wish they could be eternal.

Can This Marriage Be Saved? A Quiz

10. Why do you doubt the future of your marriage?

a. Your husband secretly opened a bank account, deposited $800 worth of freelance checks, rented an apartment, and spirited away dishes and towels, planning to disappear.

b. He said he married you because he was afraid of the future.

c. He stayed after all, but suddenly you were wildly attracted to other men, men who leapt and twisted in their pursuit of a basketball, men who casually reached up for kitchen plates, men with wild hair and long arms and intense thoughts, and your religious faith began to reconfigure itself. Some would say that it had slipped. You tell yourself that you have just let it take on a new, less severe, form.

d. "Don't leave me," your husband says as you detach yourself from your marriage after years of hanging on. He's resolved to be a better husband, but you're sure that his dissatisfaction will return eventually, and you don't think you can take it anymore, never being sure from one moment to the next where you stand.

e. Trying and trying to understand how you have ended up here, you come across a quote by Emerson: "Shallow men believe in luck . . . Strong men believe in cause and effect." You want to be strong, not shallow, but how can it be that for every effect there is a cause? Within days, your life will unroll behind you like paper towels falling downstairs. You will stop saying *who, how, why,* and start saying *because, because, because,* and it all seems as simple as those quizzes in women's magazines that you are fond of taking, except that the causes seem like they will never end. They might go on unwinding behind you your whole life.

f. You are tired of everything being about the past, tired of being paralyzed at the memory of a bunch of boys in a science class, tired of your first love's hold being tightened by the mystery of his disappearance. So you track him down, determined to find out what is so wrong with you that you drove him away, made him disappear. Why you make men disappear.

g. Your first love tells you what you somehow never knew, a fact that absolves you in an instant of years of self-blame: "I'm gay," he says, and your head goes light, all of you is light, like in the final moment before an airplane touches ground, when the body lifts slightly from the seat, levitating. Then you land gently in your life.

11. But how is it remotely possible that you never suspected that he was gay?

a. Because you were teenagers in 1970s Kansas, and no one you knew talked about this possibility. Ever. Except once he did tell you that he doubted his sexuality, and you thought it meant he didn't have any.

b. Because, he told you, he hadn't wanted to be gay, hadn't wanted to admit it.

c. Because you assumed it was normal for two shy people to take so long to kiss. You thought his nervousness was understandable and easily explained.

d. Because his many other problems seemed almost like enough to make sense of him.

e. Because you had such a talent for thinking everything was your fault.

f. Because you didn't want to know. In retrospect, it will all seem so obvious. But denial, you have discovered, can be a powerful thing.

g. Because for so many years, you weren't ready to understand how you could love someone but feel no desire.

SPEAK SOFTLY

SIX MONTHS BEFORE I meet Jon, eight months before I find out the truth about Cole, an indignant letter arrives from my mom accompanied by a pile of discarded magazines. My little brother, a senior in high school, was called out of class when it was reported that there was a weapon in his car. He was escorted to his hatchback and ordered to unlock it. A large stick was confiscated. My mother is disgusted. She says that the stick was there to hold up the hatchback door.

A news item that my mother mentions in passing catches my attention. A student at the same school had reported being raped. The school had started an investigation, then dismissed it when they found out that the girl had "engaged in prostitution."

I'm surprised at how much this letter unsettles me. Restlessly, I page through the magazines my mom has enclosed, dipping in and out of the cover stories, usually profiles of celebrities. They all had difficult childhoods, growing up "dirt poor" or in single-parent households, having trouble fitting in with peers as a result. While the general template of each story follows the star from tragedy to triumph or from heartbreak to healing, often as an aside the profiles' subjects report what they eat to maintain their trim figures: "Fat grams be damned," declares one actress who eats raw vegetables and chicken marsala for dinner, no Oreos or Cheetos in sight. A tiny actress comments that an even tinier one makes her feel like Moby Dick.

But the real point is that each of these celebrities is "finally at peace with her body—and her life," even if she calls herself "a work in progress." These subjects see their lives as fairy tales, they talk about the causes they support but emphasize their roles as mothers, they put their relationships before their careers, they take time out for perspective, and they consider balance the key to everything. I cast aside the magazines. None of these lives sound as messy as mine. Nobody is ever angry or conflicted. They are always philosophical about their struggles and choices.

When Marc gets home, he pops open a beer and reports about his day. I tell him, casually, about my mother's letter. We go upstairs to bed. I can't sleep. I keep thinking about the letter. I keep thinking about the way my mother marched down to the school and defended my little brother. My mother never marched down to the school to defend me. She laughed when I tried to tell her what was happening to me in eighth-grade science class. She said that unwanted attention meant that boys liked me. She is more angry at the idea that anyone could accuse her son of doing violence than at anything that ever happened to her daughter.

I go downstairs in the dark and lie on the couch. Turn on a lamp and look at my mom's magazines some more. Read article after article that assumes that everyone has a husband and children and likes to do crafts and cook and find the best method of cleaning a shower. It all feels so foreign to me, like this is a kind of life I can pretend to lead, but I'll always know I'm an imposter. I can disguise myself as a wife and a Good Christian and an ordinary woman who cares about cleaning products, but those disguises will never match my insides. My mother is enraged that anyone would limit the lives of her sons, but she just shrugged when I gave in to pressure to get married. Why was she okay with seeing me throw my life away?

I know this isn't entirely fair, and I feel guilty about that, but that doesn't close the floodgates that have opened unexpectedly, a whole torrent of anger surging through some barrier that I didn't know was there until it lifted and a cascade of unfamiliar emotions gush, roil, form large swirling whirlpools that threaten to suck me under.

I remember times that my mom defended my brothers, called teachers, complained to principals. I remember a time when a strange man pounded on our door, red-faced, and started yelling at my mother while gesticulating wildly at my little brother, six or seven at the time, playing in the front yard. I crept from where I was reading in the living room to listen and untangle the man's rage:

my brother had been throwing rocks into a deep ditch alongside the road, and as the man drove by in his newly washed car, muddy water had flown up to splash it. He demanded that my mother give him five dollars for another car wash. My mother refused.

After the man finally left, still seething, my mom called my older brother and me. "I want you to go out front and gather some rocks," she said, "and then, whenever you see a car coming, throw the rocks in the water and see if it's possible to intentionally splash mud on a car."

So my big brother and I, young teenagers, amused by our mother's indignant determination, aimed rocks toward the ditch, proving once and for all that it was impossible to purposely splash a passing car. Or at least proving once and for all that we were too inept to manage this feat.

Maybe, I think now, flipping pages through an article about a movie star who just gave birth and lost her baby weight in record time, it's not my mother I'm mad at, but a school administration that confiscates something as insignificant as a stick from someone's car but finds an excuse to ignore a rape. Finds a way to make it the girl's fault. I read articles about women who finally found diagnoses for obscure illnesses, women who have new outlooks on life, how-tos showing that your wardrobe can be both practical *and* sexy. Nothing about marrying the wrong person, how to leave your husband, how to survive divorce. Nothing about random, paralyzing anger and grief that flares up in the middle of the night. I take a hot shower. I recite Elizabeth Bishop's "One Art" over and over: "The art of losing isn't hard to master. . . ." I have taken to memorizing villanelles and reciting them in the shower. The rhythms of language and of the pulsating hot water soothe me.

Eventually I sleep, and in the morning I can't imagine why I'm so bothered about some insignificant thing that happened to me when I was fourteen years old. I write back to my mother. I include flippant advice to my little brother: "Tell him to speak softly," I write, "and *don't* carry a big stick."

But I'm tired of speaking softly. Tired of tiptoeing around my husband. Tired of not talking honestly about my life. And often I'm still caught by surprise by a snarled knot of feelings, like the next fall, soon before my twenty-fifth birthday, soon after I meet Jon and right before I call Cole, when I watch *West Side Story* on TV, a movie I first saw in eighth-grade music class. I freeze at a scene I don't remember: Anita delivering a message to Tony at Doc's drugstore, finding herself trapped in a mob of Jets whose verbal harassment is escalating to physical assault when Doc's arrival interrupts them and defuses the situation.

I remember what it felt like to be trapped in a crowd of boys grabbing at me and yelling profanities. I remember how agitated I felt all the time, not knowing when they were going to surround me again. "Were you raped?" friends will ask me outright in later years, as if such experiences can't really be ordeals otherwise.

Many years later, our culture will start to embrace the idea that bullying, harassment, and discrimination carry with them cumulative demoralizing effects. Data compiled by women's groups will suggest that 95 percent of sexually harassed women suffer from debilitating stress reactions, including anxiety, depression, headaches, sleep disorders, weight loss or gain, lowered self-esteem, and sexual dysfunction.

But at twenty-four, I still find my own reactions mysterious, seemingly out of proportion to the situation. It takes me until the end of *West Side Story* to stop shaking. Marc passes through the room, pauses to watch the movie for a minute, never notices that I've been transformed by one scene, but why should he notice? I look the same on the outside.

Ever since Jon came into my life, Marc is more affectionate. He stops to rub my shoulders. My free-floating anger lands on him. Why is it that the more remote, depressed, passive, and boring I am, the more he loves me?

Jon teases me about the way that, whenever anyone compliments me, I'm embarrassed. I'm afraid they'll think I believe them. I remember how often, as a teenager, I'd catch my reflection in mirrors and examine it to make sure I blended in, looked normal. I tell Jon about a sign along the highway: "Beauty Warehouse," it says. "We sell to everyone."

He doesn't find this as funny as I do.

It's Halloween, only a few days from the phone call to Cole that will change my life. I'm working as a writer in the schools at Lee Elementary in Springdale, and there's a Halloween parade. The teachers are dressed like the California Raisins as they march to "Heard It Through the Grapevine," which blares on repeat over the loudspeaker for thirty minutes while children file by, dressed like punks and French maids and Mary Poppins and a Hershey's Kiss. They have black eyes or faces painted with glittering stars. A boy in camouflage wears a bandana and makeup is smeared across his face to resemble blood and dirt. "I'm a kid just back from Vietnam," he says in a peculiarly emotionless voice when I ask him about his costume. Poor kids march defiantly, without costumes, or in their pajamas and rabbit slippers, or with coats over their heads, pretending to be headless.

I remember that early date with Marc when he was a nun and I was the devil. For seven years now, I feel like I've been wearing a disguise. Marc's wife. Happily married woman. Normal young woman. And I know, though I don't yet know how, that I'll soon be taking off those costumes, that I'll transform back into myself, whoever that is.

A year later, at Halloween, I'll dress as Miss MFA, Pageant Queen. I'll glue sequins to a tight black dress from Goodwill, make a sparkly sash, lather on makeup, tease my hair up high, and stuff my bra.

Everyone dances in the living room of the house I share with my friend Cindy, the floor so crowded that people step on my feet and my shoelaces keep coming untied. Jon and his officemate will arrive, dressed like each other. One of our classmates wears a sandwich board bearing a *New Yorker* letterhead; he's a rejection slip. Another classmate dresses as a male chauvinist pig, complete with pig snout and muddy streaks across his face. Jon's new girlfriend admires my costume. Some of the guys get drunk and try to place long-distance calls to Walker Percy and Anne Tyler. And I advocate for world peace, and when guys stare at my boobs, I say, "They're not real," and when a couple of women tell me I should wear makeup like that all the time, I laugh, knowing that I'll just wear this costume for one night and then go back to being me.

Can This Marriage Be Saved?

Answer Key

If most of your answers were A–R, you and your husband will be mature and civilized as you set each other free. Released from stress, his health will instantly improve. You will try not to feel guilty about years of flare-ups, stiff joints, rashes, restricted movement. You will help him pack. You will transport boxes to his new place. As you leave for another load, he will flick on the porch light. That light will glow in your rearview mirror as you drive away, shrinking to the size of the diamond you still wear. That porch light, not you, will greet him at night from now on.

You'll both be kind and sad. You'll talk about how you've outgrown the relationship, an easier explanation than that you were never really in love with him. You will type your own divorce papers, which require that one of you sue the other. You'll apologize profusely but secretly enjoy the power of being the one who sues him. Taking decisive action is such a relief, you'll feel inspired. You'll pick an argument on the phone. He'll get so angry, he'll hurl the receiver, then the entire phone. His line will go dead.

At 3:00 a.m., you'll meet in the parking lot of a twenty-four-hour IGA whose sign blinks steadily above your heads. You will yell at each other while he shakes the ruined phone at you, its innards a visible scramble of metal, curly cord lassoing the air, detached rotary dial frisbeeing across the lot. All at once you'll feel alive. You'll exist. You'll accuse him. To punctuate a point, he'll slam the phone's remains onto the car seat, but there is no crash, no cacophony of trapped bells, just the pathetic little ding of a fading ringer. And suddenly you'll double over laughing and laughing, and after one bewildered beat he'll join you.

And there you'll be, alive, existing, afraid of the future in the parking lot of a twenty-four-hour grocery store at 3:00 a.m., laughing and laughing.

CABIN HELPER

IN A MEMORY that seems to summarize my entire youthful marriage, I'm twenty-two years old, kneeling in the loft of a half-built cabin, a platform on stilts, by the Ninnescah River. The brown river winds through the trees while a manic wind creaks joints and whips tangled hair into my mouth. The wind scuttles a cup from lunch, hop-skipping it across the prairie below. It snarls my husband's tape measure as he climbs a ladder, nailing on the siding that I strain to hold steady. The loft tosses in the wind like a ship at the mercy of the ocean.

Now, when I relate to my daughter stories about my past, I tell her about how, as a Camp Fire Girl, I only made it to the level of Trail Seeker, and as part of the Caravan organization at the Nazarene church, I never made it beyond the initial rank of Pathfinder. I never got promoted to the second rank, Cabin Helper, much less the top rank, Homemaker. Now, looking back, this all seems symbolic to me, since I spent years seeking a trail, trying to find my path. But when I remember that cabin on the Ninnescah River, I want to say, see? I became a Cabin Helper at least briefly, after all.

Marc and I not only both have daughters named Sophie, they are both Chinese-American. A single parent, I adopted my daughter from Zhejiang Province ten years after the divorce. His daughter, and a son, are the result of a marriage to a woman from Shanghai. I don't know why he gave his daughter, five years younger than mine, the same name, except that he just happened to like it. It's a sign to me of the small and large ways we influenced each other, even if we couldn't stay married.

Being parents has rooted us in the present. "I've always lived forward," Marc writes to me. But I often find myself circling back. Unfathomably, a month ago, my daughter was the same age I was on my wedding day. And as she makes her choices, I'm always trying to figure out how to explain my own.

When I was twenty-six, I wrote in my journal, "My life is just a lot of particles floating around and I keep recombining them into different atomic structures." I tried to tell the story of my marriage many different ways. First, fictionalized, as short stories. Then in a novel manuscript. Then as a memoir. Finally, as a series of essays: trying to understand a story that's slippery, particles recombining again and again throughout my life into different atomic structures.

Because, after all, there are so many ways to tell a story.

My fearless daughter doesn't understand the terror that dominated my childhood. My daughter guffaws when

I tell her about the preschool teacher who once said, "Nancy is a very timid child." My daughter looks at me skeptically: her mom, timid? She kind of wishes I would be a little more timid, not so willing to speak up or ignore senseless rules.

As a child, though, I remember a constant sense of fear. When I was eleven, when BTK had first emerged in Wichita and murdered the Otero family, I was prone to nightmares every time a newspaper article about him appeared. Fear was a backdrop to our lives: I thought it was normal to seek reassurance in the sound of a dial phone, to carry weapons outside to get the morning newspaper. Later, I'd make Marc spend the night at my parents' house, sleeping in my little brother's bedroom, when they were away on weekends before we were married; I'd be skittish, as a new wife, when I was alone in my childhood home doing laundry. I'd be terrified when a man came to the door of our apartment to ask to use the phone. Watching the news could send me spiraling into a panic.

When I was twelve or thirteen, I dreaded adulthood, having to learn to drive and get a job, but my real fear was focused on the possibility of being murdered. All other fears were abstract. For instance, the traffic safety film shown in seventh-grade science class didn't leave me the least bit shaken; it seemed irrelevant to me, since I was years from getting my license. A car drifted into the oncoming lane, then bang! It was chaos. Here I lost track. A car spun like a pinwheel, another bounced and rolled like a basketball. Roofs collapsed, sides wadded like ads crumpled for the trash, glass crackled, webbed, exploded into sword-edged shards, doors flew from their hinges.

Or so my classmates said, tenting hands over faces, predicting nightmares, citing later an arm by the road, rain falling on the car's underbelly, wheels still spinning. Sirens, flashing, pulsating lights, then silence. A camera panning the aftermath: tire tracks in the dirt. A twisted bumper. A piece of someone's ear.

What I learned was that I couldn't see what others saw. I struggled to distinguish twigs from fingers, seashells from ears, arms from flaps of tires from snakes, blood from rain, though in my own defense, the film was in black and white.

In my journal, fourteen-year-old me described Cole as my soulmate, the love of my life. I wrote that we had a silent bond. That we were meant to be. I was giddy at my luck, at having found the one person I was predestined to be with. And then, eventually, I wondered, Why couldn't he see this? But if there was a mote in his eye, I was blind to the beam in my own. There was so much I was unable to see.

At eighteen, still convinced that he was my one and only, I would have said that he was confused, depressed, so weighed down by family issues that his vision was distorted. How did I completely miss the real nature of his struggle?

At twenty-five, when it all became clear to me, when he said to me, "Nancy, I'm gay," when I looked back and began to recast my life in that light, I was remorseful, hard on myself. I wished I'd been a better friend. When Jon asked me, "Aren't you afraid that you turn men gay?" I just rolled my eyes and said, "Are you trying to tell me something?" Jon was not, as far as I know, gay, though he eventually vaporized, coming on strong when I was married and retreating rapidly when my marriage ended. I was surprised to be heartbroken for less than three months over this, after so many years of being devastated over the loss of Cole. I came to understand how mystery can sustain grief.

In the beginning, it turned out, Cole and I had been a refuge for each other: him from his sense of being unacceptable, from the homophobic jokes and cutting comments that negated who he was, from the hostile environment he lived in to which I remained oblivious. I meanwhile found in him a sanctuary from a sense of constant threat, from boys who threw frog parts and exposed themselves in the lab room, who whistled and yelled and grabbed a fistful of my coat and reeled me in when I tried to leave the school one afternoon, just one of many incidents I've mostly forgotten that I stumble upon now in my childhood journals. I yanked away. I ran. I dreamed about Cole, who I knew was not like that.

I watched him from afar, watched him grow up, noting the deepening of his voice, the moment that his boots finally made him taller than me. He asked for my school picture when I was fifteen, before we were really dating, and later I glimpsed it in his wallet. Celebrating someone's birthday at Ferrell's ice cream parlor, I handed him the lettuce from my burger and he put it in his pocket. Such small gestures kept my dream alive. I didn't see how that photo, even that lettuce, were for him tickets to what we had been taught to believe was normality.

Not sweet, romantic gestures, after all, but efforts at survival. I can look at my past dispassionately now, so many years after my marriage ended, so many years ago that it feels like someone else's life, someone else's story. A story that I have framed and reframed again and again. I want to tell my daughter: Your story will mean different things to you during different parts of your life. It is never just one thing.

For instance, I might tell her:

When I agreed to marry Marc, I was grieving, too checked out to have any desires, sure I would never be deeply attracted to anyone else ever again. I didn't think there would ever be anyone else. Because I didn't feel the way I thought I was supposed to toward him, I was worried that I only knew how to be attracted to inaccessible men rather than truly good guys like Marc. At least all of my friends put it that way: that Marc was a "good guy."

Marc was drawn to my distance, my lack of need or desire or expectation. He could project whatever he wanted onto me, just as I'd projected what I'd wanted onto Cole.

I let him pressure me. I knew I was making a mistake.

That was one way I could tell the story. But there are others.

Marc was my boss. No one back then seemed to think there was anything wrong with that. I was afraid to say no, afraid of hurting his feelings, afraid that life at work would be unbearable, that I would be ostracized by co-workers, that I'd have to leave a job I loved. And anyway, he seemed like such a nice guy. At least everyone else was always saying so. I didn't realize then that nice guys can be predatory too.

But there's yet another side to this story. Now I look back and see that my decision was more than a caving to pressure, more than a mistake in vision, more than my sense of being beholden to a man who thought he wanted me, more than my desire to escape all of the violence in the world: car wrecks and wars, the casual demeaning behavior of junior high boys, rapes and murders, the terrifying possibilities. In fact, I'm surprised to see in my college journals how happy I was during the year that Marc and I were engaged. I felt safe and loved, happy and hopeful. I felt secure enough to start having expectations again. But there were warning signs that I ignored. A month before the wedding, he wanted to take a three-week vacation to visit his brother. I thought he should get a job. He was angry at me. All of the invitations were addressed, but he wanted to postpone the wedding so that he could go on his trip. I refused to acknowledge any of these red flags, his cold feet, my own doubts.

Every failure, I thought back then, was my fault. Women who made excuses not to have sex with their husbands were called "frigid," but then, the focus of medical studies and media reports tended to be on men's satisfaction, not women's, with little acknowledgment that a man could put forth effort to enhance a female partner's experience. Perhaps recognition of that on both of our parts would have helped. Still, I have no definitive answer about why this was such a difficult part of my marriage any more than I can explain why I was so blind about Cole being gay.

I would go on to make much more careful choices, not wanting to find myself in another situation as wrong for me as my marriage was. But mistakes are impossible to avoid, of course. At least the subsequent relationships that weren't right for me were short-lived ones. Still, I made mistakes, found myself in jobs and places that were unsuited to me before I found the jobs and people that were. And I made the great leap of faith of adopting my daughter as a single parent, knew to follow my intuition despite my fear, and made the best decision of my life.

In my memory, I'm clinging to a flimsy cabin frame while the hiss of the wind rises like an oncoming tide. I've been married just a couple of years. For the last few weeks, Marc has been building this cabin on his uncle's property while I work at the front desk of a company that owns greasy spoons throughout Wichita. I answer phones and tally receipts and each night I half-listen to Marc report on his progress. He talks about constructing a wooden form, pouring the concrete foundation. He talks about batter boards, corner stakes, subfloors, frames. This is the first time that I've seen his handiwork, this windy day that I help with the siding. I'm awed that he has built this by himself, from nothing. That he understands all of this stuff about siding and roofs and foundations.

At twenty-two, all I know about foundations comes from a Bible story in which the wise man built his house upon the rock, the foolish one on sand. Our marriage, I know, is built on sand and fear, and the walls will come tumbling down.

Even when you walk away from a religious upbringing, as I did eventually, these Bible stories are still deeply embedded in your interpretation of the world. I still remember being taken, in Sunday school as a child, by the story of how Adam named the animals. What power he had each time God brought him another beast of the field or bird of the air. Whatever Adam called each living creature, that was its name. He named the cats and dogs, elephants and hamsters, frogs and chickens and cockroaches. I imagined the power of giving things their names, how applying names to things makes the world less chaotic, how it suddenly makes sense.

And while mystery and uncertainty are unavoidable, there are answers to some questions I once thought were unanswerable. Such life-changing moments tended to begin with a phone call. "I'm gay," Cole said to me, and those words brought my life into focus like a new pair of glasses, the way you put them on and suddenly see that leaves are more than a green blur, but have sharp, blade-like tips or rough, saw-like edges, or soft, feathery shapes. You see the cracks in walls, the spears of grass, the spiraling blooms on yellow wildflowers. Before, you'd had only a vague inkling of what you were missing.

In 2005, my mother called me. "They caught BTK," she said, and the serial killer who'd terrorized East Wichita throughout my childhood ceased to represent all of the ambiguity and uncertainty we sometimes just have to learn to live with. For days I remained glued to CNN, shocked that the bogeyman was a real person after all rather than some nebulous evil force, as mesmerized as if Bigfoot had been nabbed. BTK had a name, and that alone changed my outlook, my belief that there were many things it was possible to understand, after all, if always incompletely.

But that day in the cabin's loft, poised high up there on the edge of a platform surrounded by absence, by empty spaces, as I peer through the frame, poised on the edge of my future, I'm still missing so much information. Rocked and jolted by wind, I fear that I'll be flung overboard, landing among heaving wildflowers, clusters of purple, coils of yellow. The wind blows so hard that the clouds scatter and then reconvene, casting shadows on the frenzied green and white grass. I pull the siding tight, hanging on with white-knuckled might as if for both of us: me in the loft, Marc on his precarious ladder, barely bothering to hang on."

Throughout my adult life, my mother prayed for me constantly. She was convinced that I wasn't going to go to heaven. She didn't know why I couldn't be like Marie Osmond, who according to women's magazines routinely discussed her faith with her mother. My mother couldn't see that I had retained philosophies that I thought were important, lessons about kindness and compassion and love, while discarding sexism, intolerance, judgment, and in particular an outsized obsession with sexual virtue.

It took me a long time to leave my marriage and an even longer time to give up on churches. A classmate told one of my friends, when Marc and I separated, "She shouldn't leave him. He's the most interesting thing about her." I rolled my eyes at the bizarre misogyny of that statement, but secretly I wondered, What if that was true?

In Fayetteville after my divorce, I sometimes attended Episcopal services. The next year, I moved to Missouri and visited a church with a thriving singles organization, but I couldn't stomach the big TV screens and megachurch insincerity. I visited a FOCAS group, which stood for Fellowship of Christian Adult Singles, where I was the youngest woman by far. There were some country western hymns and a five-minute fellowship period where members circulated and hugged each other, reminding each other that these were the only hugs they'd get all week. Then the pastor, the only married person in the building, delivered a sermon titled, "Should single people go on—or just give up?"

I didn't go back. I went to a Quaker meeting and sat in silence for an hour. Eventually, I took a job at a church-connected college and every last vestige of interest in organized religion died in the face of all of the judgmental attitudes I'd been trying my whole adult life to escape. By the time I became a parent, I had no plans to send my child to Sunday school. It's hard for me now to remember quite why religion had such a deep hold on me, why it was as strong a factor in the duration of my marriage as my fear of being alone, as fierce a component as was my blindness to my own strength.

Often I'd been blind, even as far back as when I was ten or eleven, the time my aunt and uncle followed the Goodyear Blimp through Kansas City in their station wagon. My cousins stabbed fingers toward the sky, saying, "See? See? Don't you see?" I didn't. I had a headache and was tired of futilely scanning the clouds. It felt as if my cousins' insistent gesturing, their determination to make me see, was all a conspiracy to make me feel inadequate. Later, I had trouble differentiating, in *Star Wars*, shapes whirling in space. I couldn't figure out who was fighting who, or why the princess wore those big earphones that turned out to be her hairdo.

This was not an adequate excuse for all I failed to see, much less decipher. Sadness flashing across Cole's face, the meaning of the suicide ritual he described to me, the time he narrowly avoided a brutal attack by some boys in the hall after school, his angry fist battering a locker. In my defense, it was the '70s, it was Kansas, and I was busy studying the sweet labyrinth of his ear.

I missed so much. I was unaware of the prevalence of sexual harassment in my school, probably in most schools at the time, until, a few years ago, I found myself riveted by a Facebook discussion by former junior high classmates of creepy teachers who made inappropriate comments to students and, in at least one case, had a habit of cornering them in supply closets. I remember how I maintained banter with other male teachers and administrators, and recorded numerous occasions that male teachers asked me for hugs. At the time, it seemed harmless. Other girls report that it wasn't. That for them, it escalated into more traumatic behavior.

I tell my daughter how much the world has changed. When I was eleven, when the Otero family was killed, there were no computers whose disks could be traced and no way to track DNA evidence. Technological leaps forward were what finally led to BTK's capture. My journals are full of outdated references. Cole said to me once, "I remember when I'd see a toy advertised on TV, and then I'd get it for Christmas, and I was always so excited because it was in color." Dating Marc, I described how someone in a movie theater lit a cigarette, how the light contracted twice like a quick heartbeat, then was gone. I drew a sketch of how I was going to arrange our house in Pratt, Kansas, including a clothesline in the backyard. I described the kittens poking their heads through the holes in the middle of records. Now, my daughter takes for granted that everything is in color, that no one smokes in theaters. We use a dryer, stream our music. "Me too," people post on Facebook. We no longer so easily accept what horrifies me now.

Things change, attitudes change, the world changes. My daughter can follow links like "26 things that look like butts" on the Internet and view double egg yolks, plump Valentine's candy, malformed peaches, radishes, tomatoes.

This is just another iteration for the possible ways we can mistake one thing for another.

I have always done that, remember how I mistook Cole's hesitation for shy desire, his sadness for something I could fix, his wreckage for the same mangled metal of adolescence from which we all had to extract ourselves, heaving awkward bodies through those gaps left by unhinged doors like portals to another world. Him slipping through, somehow intact, disappearing from my flawed sight.

That day in the cabin's loft, I am still years from understanding Cole or this marriage I'm still clinging to. The wind's roaring drowns out the ringing of nails as a wall rises around me. It erases objects directly below: the chainsaw, sawhorse, triangles and rectangles of wood scraps. More of the world vanishes as the wall grows: the long prairie grass, the feathery asparagus fields, the thin dark line of the Ninnescah, green patches, brambling blurs—sand plums, wild grapes, poison ivy.

I'm a few years from encountering the Audre Lorde quote, "The master's tools will never dismantle the master's house." I have no clue how I'll be able to dismantle this marriage, or how much, over subsequent years, I'll change my views of sexual politics. Right now, I'm still far more attuned to my husband's satisfaction than my own, and the way he chafes at the restrictions of marriage. I long to close my eyes, to go on not seeing, as I crouch behind a wall that rises little by little, blocking out the horizon, stilling the wind. Marc fills the spaces. Numbs the roar. Calms the shuddering.

Isn't this a kind of love? I wonder. Not tempestuous like my first love or the windy prairie outside. Not magical like the catfish that, according to lore, fling themselves out of the Ninnescah to bite wild grapes off the vines. Not wild like the long grass that shivers the way my skin did under Cole's touch. Bracing myself against the wind, trying to stay firm, drains me, leaves me drowsy.

This is love, I convince myself. This calm. This protection.

I build my own wall against seeing that maybe this won't be enough in the long run. My own wall against this glimpse of how love ends. Wind so tamed you forget its power. Losses so slow you might not heed them.

Gone, little by little, piece by piece: sagging tool belt, reckless fingers. Lip-pinched nails, tender eyes. And then the treetops. Then the sky.

AUTHOR'S NOTE

WRITING ACKNOWLEDGMENTS FOR a memoir about childhood and young adulthood is a daunting task, particularly when that memoir has taken many years to write: there are so many people who contributed to the process that it's impossible to thank everyone. Many, many people offered feedback, friendship, insights, and wisdom that assisted me during both the living of the experiences of this book and the writing of it.

I owe a huge debt to Anna Smith, who talked me through this process many times over the years, suggesting when I was discouraged a few years ago that I try breaking down this story into individual essays before integrating them into a book. During recent years I also benefited from feedback from Livingston Alexander, Karen Bell, Karyl Anne Fischer, Darlene Goetzman, Liza Greville, Sara King, Lee Martin, Carol Newman, and Dani Weber. Several generous friends and writers stepped in to comment on drafts of this when I was working on a final revision; most of them didn't know each other, but their comments created an awesome tag team that led me to an overhaul of the manuscript. Thank you Elizabeth Dalton, Lisa Knopp, Eddie Lueken, and Jody Lisberger.

Childhood friends including Shauna Viele and Ruth Yoon have offered unflagging support for my writing and their own supportive memories of these years. My ex-husband has always been gracious about appearing in my work, even if his take on these events would be entirely different, and he was equally gracious about giving me permission to appear in photographs in these pages. I also want to acknowledge the high school boyfriend I refer to as Cole, since I don't want to intrude on his privacy any more than that; it makes me enormously happy to see the good lives that both Marc and "Cole" have made for themselves and I'm grateful for the ways that knowing both of them shaped me.

I have too many great friends, colleagues, and former students at both the University of Pittsburgh at Bradford and the Spalding University School of Creative and Professional Writing to thank by name, but I owe special thanks to Marietta Frank, friend and librarian extraordinaire who can always unearth any resource I need in record time, Gaj and Rekha Gajanan for *Jeopardy!* breaks and chocolate, and Josh Groffman, who lent his knowledge of music to help me with some directions for these essays. Thanks to Jeff Guterman, chair of the Division of Communication and the Arts at Pitt-Bradford, and my energetic and inspiring colleagues. Sena Jeter Naslund, Kathleen Driskell, Karen Mann, and everyone at Spalding have provided boundless support and inspiration, and literally hundreds of students and faculty there have heard me read from these pieces over the years and offered feedback and encouragement. Friends and workshop colleagues in the University of Nebraska PhD program, the Missouri State English Department, and the University of Arkansas MFA program were key in the development of many of these pieces as well. Special thanks to my dear friends Cindy Vincent and Karen Hindhede and for the generosity of my friend and colleague Lori Jakiela, whose books everyone should read right now.

My dad took many of the photographs here, and I owe extra special thanks to Bernie Picklo, whose enthusiasm always overcomes my tech anxiety and who has been generous with his time and expertise many times, most recently in helping me with the process of including photographs. The majority of the photographs are from my private collection. Exceptions are the Pratt water towers and the Bosch painting, which were available for commercial use on Google Images; for the image of Carlson Terrace, I owe thanks to Geoffrey Stark and Special Collections at the University of Arkansas Libraries for locating this photograph and giving me permission to use it. Thanks also to Trish Vandervelden for agreeing to allow me to include photographs of her, and to the *Pratt Tribune* for permission to reprint material.

I am indebted to Kimberly Marcott Weinberg for all of her PR work, Dr. Steve Hardin and the Office of Academic Affairs at Pitt-Bradford for faculty development grants that assisted with developing some of these pieces, the Pennsylvania Council on the Arts for an individual artist grant that nudged me forward, and editors who published these pieces and offered valuable feedback, including Dianne Aprile, Peter Field, Bret Lott, Brenda Miller, Ron Mitchell, and Ian Morris. Some of the chapters in this book were originally published in very different form in the following:

"The Garden of Earthly Delights" and "Honeymoon Reservations," *Mud Season Review* (published together as one essay and nominated for *Best of the Net*)

"Ways to Tell a Story," *Florida Review* (also named a Notable Essay of 2017 by *Best American Essays*)

"Facts about the Moon," *Timberline Review*

"First Love: A Curriculum Guide," *Potomac Review*

"Before and After," *Crazyhorse*

"With Abandon," *Placeholder Review*

"Breathing on Your Own," *Punctuate*

"Metamorphosis," *Southern Indiana Review* (also named a Notable Essay of 2018 by *Best American Essays*)

"Flight," *Louisville Review*

"Can This Troubled Marriage Be Saved: A Quiz," *Bellingham Review*

"Cabin Helper," *Watershed Review*

I've been privileged to work with the University of Missouri Press four times now, and want to thank everyone who worked on this book, including Gary Kass, Mary Conley, Megan Casey-Sparrius, Robin Rennison, Drew Griffith, and Barbara Smith-Mandell.

And finally, thank you to Steve Cheney, who is such a gift, and to Sophie McCabe, who I know now: every event of my life was preparing me to be your mom.